WINE TASTER'S GUIDE

Wine Taster's Guide

Guide

Drink and Learn with
30 Wine Tastings

JOE ROBERTS

ROCKRIDGE PRESS

Interior and Cover Designer: Sean Doyle
Art Producer: Sue Bischofberger
Editor: Pam Kingsley
Production Editor: Rachel Taenzler

Photography © DMP1/iStock, cover; MarkSwallow/iStock, p. ii; CarlosAndreSantos/iStock, p. x; Brunomsbarreto/iStock, p. 13; Sven Sauder/iStock, p. 18; laughingmango/iStock, pp. 22, 33, 46, and 154; Coco Casablanca/iStock, p. 23; FreeProd/Alamy Stock Photo, p. 24; Gibson Outdoor Photography/Alamy Stock Photo, p. 28; Lorenza photography/Alamy Stock Photo, p. 31; eurotravel/iStock, p. 35; JMichl/iStock, p. 38; EyeEm/Alamy Stock Photo, p. 39; ueuaphoto/iStock, p. 44; Leonsbox/iStock, p. 50; PIXEL to the PEOPLE/shutterstock, pp. 53 and 148; Eckhard Supp/Alamy Stock Photo, p. 56; Chris Mellor/Alamy Stock Photo, p. 61; izikMd/iStock, p. 62; Josef Mohyla/iStock, p. 65; Kloeg008/iStock, pp. 66 and 144; Kondor83/iStock, p. 72; OceanProd/iStock, p. 73; Daan Kloeg/shutterstock, p. 75; JAM WORLD IMAGES/Alamy Stock Photo, p. 81; seraficus/iStock, p. 84; Tiago_Fernandez/iStock, p. 96; cristianoalessandro/iStock, p. 98; Maudib/iStock, p. 103; Sanny11/iStock, p. 106; estivillml/iStock, p. 116; THEPALMER/iStock, p. 121; tomwachs/iStock, p. 122; samvaltenbergs/iStock, p. 125; cristianl/iStock, p. 129; Susup/iStock, p. 132; Split Second Stock/iStock, p. 134; abriendomundo/iStock, p. 136; lovleah/iStock, p. 139; nazar_ab/iStock, p. 142; michalzak/iStock, p. 156; Mark Dunn/Alamy Stock Photo, p. 165; Larisa Blinova/Alamy Stock Photo, p. 173; and Guille Faingold/Stocksy, p. 178 Maps and illustrations © 2020 Claire Rollet Wine label on page 124 courtesy of Rodney Strong Vineyards

ISBN: Print 978-1-64611-960-8 | eBook 978-1-64611-961-5
R0

To Mom, because she's awesome

CONTENTS

INTRODUCTION

"So . . . how did you become a wine expert?"

If I had a nickel for every time I've been asked that question, I might have enough to buy one bottle of 1945 Romanée-Conti. In traveling the world and writing about fine wine for over a decade, that question is almost always the one I'm asked no matter where I am, what I'm tasting, or who's with me.

The bad news is that the answer is pretty boring. With the possible exception of Hugh Hefner, no one pops out of the womb wearing a smoking jacket, bearing a wry smile, and holding an encyclopedic knowledge of fine wine. You have to work at it. As Malcolm Gladwell wrote, if you spend ten thousand hours doing anything, you're going to get really good at it.

The good news? It takes far less time to learn how to effectively taste wine and to become an expert in something far more important: figuring out what you personally enjoy and why. It's a step that, in my experience, few wine lovers ever take.

One of the alluring things about wine is that it's fun to drink. But it's even more fun to drink wine mindfully. That's when the real learning—about wine and about your own tastes—happens. Anyone can plop down cash to buy wine with a favorable critic's review: fewer can taste a wine on its own merits and tell you what they're tasting, why they're tasting it, and why they personally like (or hate!) it.

That's where this book comes in.

This wine guide will help you learn about what you're tasting and why it tastes that way. Along the way, we'll demystify the esoteric topic of wine a bit, by deepening your appreciation and understanding about it. More important, you'll learn about your own likes and dislikes when it comes to the world's most amazing adult beverage—something that's far more important than an expert's quality assessment.

We'll explore things like why different grapes and different wine regions provide different tasting experiences, and why the same grape from different areas can end up making wines that taste completely different. The emphasis will be on the really important stuff: why that wine that you're drinking smells and tastes the way that it does.

How This Book Works

Because this is a book focused on tasting wine, you'll find 30 themed tastings sprinkled throughout, organized by chapter and related directly to the topics that are being tackled on the pages where they appear. These tastings are the fastest way to increase your wine tasting IQ, by getting your hands (well, actually, your tongue) dirty.

We'll explore how we perceive wine, from grape to glass, starting with the mechanics of how we smell and taste. We'll discuss how different grape varieties affect the texture and flavor of wines made from them and what happens during the winemaking process to craft the vinous magic that eventually passes our lips. We'll journey through the world's major wine-producing countries (including how to navigate their labels) and explore why their traditions, grapes, climates, and winemaking practices impact a wine's taste. Finally, you'll learn how to organize your own tastings to maximize the learning potential in each sip (with advice on wine buying, matching food and wine, and general wine "care and maintenance" provided along the way).

In other words, we're going to cover a lot of ground. While we can't tackle everything about wine in a book that's under 1,000 pages, we've packed as many of the practical tips and tidbits and as much of the learning from my decade of experience traversing the wine world into this book as we could. While you can skip around the various chapters (and use them as a quick and handy reference guide for your wine explorations), you'll get the most out of this book if you read it over time, cover to cover, pausing to do the tastings as you progress. (I promise, this will be some of the best "homework" you will have ever been assigned in your entire life.)

About the Wine Tastings

Take it from someone (me) who's had to study just about every wine textbook in existence—there's only so much reading that anyone can do about wine, and sooner or later you have to get wine into your mouth to really appreciate it. To that end, there are 30 tastings included in this book. Each tasting contains four to six wines on average, meant to be tasted in the order in which they're listed, and all of them themed to show you how a certain aspect (like grape variety, growing region, or winemaking style) impacts wine flavor. While they're definitely entertaining, all of the tastings have a purpose (okay, I did sneak one in there that's just for fun), and they'll prove essential in helping to make the information in this book more real to you, as you taste and smell your way across the world of wine. You'll find a handy list of all the included tastings on page 179.

A quick word about the wines that I've selected: I have tried to include wines that are tasty, well-made, reasonably affordable, readily available, and good "ambassadors" for their grape, region, and/or style. There are so many wines in the world that it would be impossible to include recommendations that are available to everyone, everywhere. The wine market is simply too diverse and competitive (and, some would argue, overregulated) for us to do that. If you can't locate a wine for some of this book's tastings, don't sweat it; you should be able to find substitutes for a grape, region, or style without too much hassle. (You can also enlist the help of the friendly staff at your favorite wine retail shop.) If you're based in the United States and are looking for wines made in America, don't forget that in many states you can order wines directly from the producer. Focus on what the tastings are meant to teach and reveal, rather than on having to do that with specific wines in hand.

Finally, remember that there are no shortcuts to acquiring wine tasting experience, so go at your own pace. Savor, sip, and discover mindfully, and you'll be well on your way to becoming your own personal wine tasting expert.

Cheers!

CHAPTER 1

TASTING 101

Wines are kind of like hamburgers. Seriously. There's a difference between enjoying a Whopper versus a grass-fed gourmet burger. That doesn't mean that the fast food burger is *bad*. In fact, it can be a real tasty bargain. It just means that there's a quality (and price) jump between them, one that is noticeable even if you're not trained to tell the difference.

It's almost the same thing with wine, except the stakes (spending your hard-earned dollars) are higher. To embark on a lifetime of wine-drinking pleasure, you don't need to become an expert in wine (that's my job); you need to become an expert in what you *like* in wine. To do that, you need to drink more mindfully. To drink more mindfully, you need to pay attention to what you're tasting. And when it comes to wine, tasting mindfully means following your nose . . . and getting scientifically geeky for a minute or two. In the next section, we will explore in detail how we smell and taste. Along the way, we'll learn about how we detect some aromas only after we taste wine and why sniffing a wine can trigger strong emotional connections, or even stir past memories.

The Factors That Impact a Wine's Flavor

While we'll go into these in more detail later in the book, it's helpful to have an overview of what makes a wine taste and smell the way that it does. Here's a quick list of the elements that determine a wine's aroma and flavor profile. As you'll see, this goes far beyond just the variety of grapes used and extends throughout the winemaking and aging processes.

- Grape variety (usually responsible for a wine's primary fruit flavors)

- Where the grapes are grown and how they're farmed

- How the wine is made

- Aging (whether a wine is aged in steel tanks, oak barrels, bottles, or other vessels, or even aged at all)

The Science of the Sniff

Most of how we experience wine is through our sense of smell, so understanding how we smell might be *the* most important first step in understanding how to taste wine. Let's take a look at the science of how we sniff.

THE PROCESS OF SMELL

It might seem counterintuitive to kick off a tasting primer by talking about smelling things, but your nose (well, technically, your olfactory system) is responsible for up to 80 percent of your perception of taste. In a very real way, smelling *is* tasting. We smell both directly through our nose (orthonasal) and through our mouths (retronasal).

Before you get too skeptical about the human mammal's ability to detect odors versus, say, a dog, bear in mind that a 2014 study showed that people can potentially distinguish one *trillion* different odors (and that was estimated to be on the low side), some in incredibly tiny concentrations. So, while many other animals outperform humans when it comes to olfaction, overall, we're no slouches in the sense of smell department (which is a very good thing for our enjoyment of wine!).

Your nose is just the beginning of your built-in smelling apparatus, and it exists in part to channel odors toward the olfactory receptors in your nasal cavity (located above the roof of your mouth). Aroma compounds bind to those receptors, which are grouped together in what's called the glomerular layer. Those glomeruli (basically, a collection of nerve endings) are an important way station en route to your brain, because they help organize information from about ten million olfactory receptor neurons. Each glomerulus gets its input mostly from neurons that are linked to similar olfactory receptors, which means that they are pretty well organized and help us logically break down the massive amount of data revealing to us how our world (and our wine) smells, before that information even gets to our brains.

Olfactory System

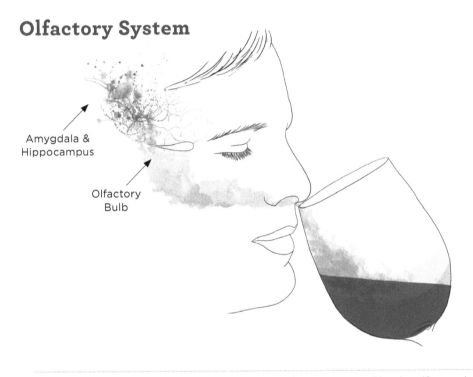

Amygdala & Hippocampus

Olfactory Bulb

When inhaled, wine's volatile aromatic compounds are processed by the olfactory bulb, which communicates with the brain's emotional (amygdala) and memory (hippocampus) areas, impacting what you perceive as aroma and taste.

The next stop on the smell train is the olfactory bulb. This amazing little natural gadget has five layers, of which the glomerular layer is just a part. The details of the olfactory bulb are not only beyond the scope of this book but so far have proven to be beyond the scope of modern science. While we know much about how it's structured, scientists don't yet fully understand exactly how the olfactory bulb functions. Because of the large amount of neural connections within it, we know that there is a lot of potential information-filtering happening in the olfactory bulb when we take a sniff.

The communication between the olfactory bulb and your brain isn't just one-way; there's top-down information being sent back to the bulb from your brain when you smell. With each sniff, your olfactory organ is most likely discriminating between different odors, enhancing the sensitivity of certain odor detectors (when you focus attention on a particular smell), and taking some of the smell-processing load off of your "higher" brain (so that it can focus on more complex thinking regarding what you're sniffing). Most of this work is done in the "blink" of a sniff, even before your conscious brain is aware that it's happening.

A VOLATILE SITUATION: WHAT MAKES UP A WINE'S AROMA

Now that we have a good idea of *how* we smell, let's talk about *what* we smell.

All wine is a stop on a continuum. On one end, there's fermented grape juice. On the other, there's vinegar. Wine is the magic that happens in between, when just the right amount of air triggers the right amount of chemistry. Our enjoyment of wine is based on how we experience that chemistry. The challenge is that the chemistry is so complex (even for our impressive noses and brains) that we have to do some interpretation, which can be confusing for those just starting to learn about wine.

Here's an example. If I mention in a wine review that an Australian Shiraz's aroma is redolent of blueberries, I don't mean that any blueberries were actually harmed in the making of that wine. What I mean is that the closest thing that our brains will get to understanding that particular aroma compound in the Shiraz is that it reminds us of blueberries. (More on the brain's role in all of this is coming up later in the chapter.) We're not actually smelling blueberries, but the brain is doing what it considers the next best thing: reinterpreting the complex aroma that it *doesn't* know into something that it already *does* know.

But what, exactly, is it that's *smelling* like a blueberry to your brain in the first place?

That would be what is known as a volatile compound. These compounds evaporate from the wine and are then suspended on the surface of the wine and the glass. Without them, wine wouldn't smell like much of anything. Volatile compounds develop from all aspects of a wine's creation, including the grape variety itself and how the wine is made. The compounds are called "volatile" because they vaporize in contact with air; this is why we can pick them up when we sniff.

One of the reasons that wine is so amazingly complex is that there are many, many of these volatile compounds in any given wine. They range from fruity (via esters and thiols) to earthy (geosmin) to vanilla-like (lactones) to floral (terpenes—which are also found in marijuana) and herbaceous (pyrazines), and that's just the tip of the iceberg. The combination of these compounds, in varying levels of intensity, is largely responsible for each wine's unique aroma profile. How many volatile compounds does a wine have? No one knows for sure. Some studies have put the number into the forties for a single grape variety, while others suggest that even the most basic wine has twenty or more volatile compounds.

Now you know why we swirl wine in the glass (to vaporize the volatile compounds) and decant (aerate) a younger wine (to expose more of its surface area—and thus its volatile compounds—to air). It's to help release a wine's grip on all of those fabulous aromas.

AROMA VS. BOUQUET

While we tend to use the terms *aroma* and *bouquet* interchangeably, often the terms are employed differently by wine pros. *Aroma* is used in wine criticism to describe a smell provided by the grape variety itself (such as blueberries in Syrah), while *bouquet* includes aromas that come from the fermentation process or aging, in oak or in bottle (such as hints of cedar in oak-aged wines, or truffles in a bottle-aged Pinot Noir). You may also come across the terms *primary*, *secondary*, and *tertiary* in describing wine aromas. Those usually refer to smells derived from the grape variety, fermentation processes, and aging, respectively.

The Science of the Sip

Now it's time to take a look at what goes on when that wine passes our lips.

THE PROCESS OF TASTE

You're probably thinking, "Okay, our sense of smell is really complicated, but taste is way easier, right? There's sweet, sour, salty, bitter, and umami taste buds, that all sit in different parts of your tongue. Easy stuff!"

Sorry, but your sense of taste is just as complex as your sense of smell, though for different reasons, and this plays a big part in how you perceive a wine. It also happens to involve every aspect of your palate, from your tongue all the way down to your esophagus (and even brings your nose back into it).

Of course, you have taste buds (between 2,000 to 4,000 on average) for those famous five flavor categories, but they are *all over* your tongue, and aren't exclusively arranged in zones as was once commonly thought. Some people have more taste buds, some fewer, and that difference can in turn cause differences in how individuals perceive the intensity of various tastes (especially bitter flavors). You also have taste buds on your epiglottis, in your sinuses, and all along the upper portion of your esophagus, all of which can pick up nuances of flavors.

You cannot see your taste buds but you can see the papillae (the tongue's small, rounded bumps) on which they sit. Adding to the complexity, there are three different types of papillae and they all affect our perception of taste. We also experience the gustatory sensations of drinking wine such as the impact of its warming alcohol or bitter tannins—more on this later—a little bit differently from person to person.

Does this mean that no two tasters are exactly alike? Yes, that's exactly what it means. And it's part of the reason why not everyone loves the same kinds of wines.

While we can't expect different people to taste things in exactly the same way, we can get close, and *most* people will tend to agree on flavors even if they perceive their intensity and textures a bit differently. (Otherwise, we'd never get the judges to agree on awarding a medal in a wine competition!)

For example, you might love the taste and rough feeling of stone-ground mustard, while I prefer good old-fashioned smooth yellow; neither of us is *wrong*, we're just *different*. This is why it's so important for you to understand what you personally like (and dislike) when it comes to tasting wine. After all, if I give an "A" grade review to an $80 bottle of Chardonnay and say that it has pure flavors of white peach, and you happen to loathe the flavor of white peaches, then you're much better off spending your money on eight bottles of a $10 wine that you really love. The important thing to understand here is that, while we might both taste white peaches from that Chardonnay, we might experience certain aspects of the intensity and texture of that same wine a bit differently and that will have a big impact on how much we personally enjoy (or hate) that wine.

Your entire palate plays another important role in tasting wine (or any food), in that it communicates texture. Texture is probably the most overlooked aspect of wine, and yet it plays a big part in how we perceive it and gives a wine most of its "personality." A wine high in acidity will feel perky—almost electric—on your tongue. A rich, higher-alcohol wine will give a perception of roundness, weight, and "seriousness" in your mouth.

Finally, once a wine hits your tongue, it vaporizes even more of its volatile compounds, which means that tasting a wine reveals more of its smells (which you then experience retronasally).

PALATE

Wine geeks like me love to use the word "palate." It might be more accurate to say that we love to overuse it. For the most part, palate refers to two different things when it comes to wine tasting.

First, a wine is described as having certain flavors, textures, and other characteristics "on the palate." In this context, palate is shorthand for describing those characteristics of a wine once it's in your mouth.

The second use of "palate" refers to an individual person's ability to discern quality and different flavors and aromas in a wine. In that case, we might say that a person has "a good palate," meaning that they are an experienced taster. Anyone can further develop their palate through experience, study, and (most important) tasting.

THIS IS YOUR BRAIN ON WINE

What our brains do with all of the fabulous taste information collected by our olfactory system and our mouths when drinking wine is fascinating in its own right, and explains why complex beverages like wine evoke such powerful emotions that move us to talk, write, learn, and debate about them.

First, our olfactory system doesn't communicate directly with our conscious brain. Instead of talking to the thalamus (which is the gatekeeper to conscious thought in the brain), the olfactory bulb first sends messages to the amygdala (which plays a key role in processing emotions) and the hippocampus (which is involved in learning and memory). Additionally, information on odors is stored in our long-term memory. This is probably why aromas can trigger such strong emotional responses in us, or recall memories associated with certain smells (grandma's apple pie, anyone?). Wine, with its panoply of aromatic complexity, speaks directly to our emotions, and provides a stimulating work-out for our sensory perception. No wonder so many people fall in love with the stuff.

Once our conscious brain gets involved, we've already processed a ton of information about a wine's aromas and flavors and associated them almost instantly with emotions and memories. Now it's time for that higher-level processing to figure out what we're tasting. The trouble is, as rich as the language processing is in our heads, we simply lack the terminology to describe the potential trillion odor combinations that we might be experiencing. So wine also gets our creative juices flowing, as our minds work to associate the beautiful onslaught of complex smells with things that we have encountered before (flowers, oak, fruits, vegetables, smoke, and on and on and on).

In a way, wine is brain food; if we focus on it, it provides an opportunity for our brains to engage in a fun intellectual matching game as we try to interpret it. It's also soul food, in that when drinking it, we connect directly with our emotions and past experiences.

How to Taste a Wine

When the wine business gets grief about being too stuffy and full of itself, the act of tasting is almost always the target. And it's usually a bum rap, because most wine—even during critical analysis and wine competitions—is tasted without a whole lot of fanfare or pretentiousness.

You don't need to do much to taste wine more mindfully; you just need to slow your roll and think about each step of the tasting experience as it's happening. At no point in the tasting process does a big deal need to be made, unless you're like me and you get so psyched about what you're tasting that you feel compelled to immediately share how great it is . . . but this isn't a book about self-control issues. There are only five aspects to tasting wine, and each one is pretty simple. Delving into them is worth a moment or two, because it's helpful to understand *why* each step is important. Just think of a wine as a teacher, and you're the student—pay attention, and you'll be learning something new in no time.

(continued on page 12) »

Tasting Wine

Look

Swirl

Smell

Taste

The first four steps of tasting wine are followed by the final step, considering what you've experienced.

THE LANGUAGE OF TASTING

Because wine can evoke such strong emotions in us when we taste, describing how a wine "feels" can be challenging. When trying to capture wine's more elusive impressions, wine pros are fond of using terminology that can seem confusing at first. Here's a key to translating some of those "emotional shorthand" descriptors.

Aggressive: This usually refers to a wine's aromas, tannins, acidity, or carbonation (in sparkling wine). It means that the wine presents an aspect in an intense and noticeable way.

Austere: Can also be described as "reserved" or "steely." These are acidic wines that are difficult to drink young and don't show much fruit flavor or aroma, often requiring years before they open up.

Body: A wine's body is its textural "weight" in your mouth. Just as some foods feel "heavier" (like steak) or "lighter" (like lettuce) as you chew them, wines can give similar impressions when tasted. Generally, a wine's body is a result of a combination of factors including its alcohol and acidity content. Lighter-bodied wines (usually under 12.5 percent alcohol) feel lighter in the mouth. Medium-bodied wines (typically 12.5 percent to 13.5 percent alcohol) feel balanced. Full-bodied wines (over 13.5 percent alcohol) feel fuller, richer, and heavier.

Bold: Most often used when describing fruit flavors. It means that the fruit is a dominant flavor when tasting the wine.

Bright: This refers to a wine's acidity and fruitiness and means that it feels energetic and mouthwatering.

Chewy: Describes fruit flavors and tannins that make you feel as if you could "chew" them because of their substantial presence in the mouth.

Crisp: Most often refers to acidity in white wines; a wine that gives the mouthwatering sensation of biting into a crisp, acidic fruit (like an apple).

Dense: A wine (usually a big red) that has high levels of concentration in its aromas and flavors. (The term "extracted" is sometimes also used.)

Elegant: Referring to either the nose or the palate (or both), we use this term for a wine that feels particularly well-balanced, with its various aspects coming together in harmony. You might also see "refined" used in a similar way.

Floral: Evoking flowers. Sometimes, generic terms such as "blossom" or "white flowers" are used. Other times, the floral aromas can be very specific; if so, we usually just mention the exact flower (like jasmine, rose petals, orange blossoms, or violets).

Grippy: Used to describe very tannic wines that "grip" your mouth and gums as you taste them.

Jammy: Evoking flavors and/or aromas of fruit jam (these can be either delicious or off-putting, depending on the wine).

Juicy: A wine with fruit flavors that feel fresh (like biting into freshly picked fruit).

Nose: A shorthand term for describing how a wine smells in the glass (the totality of its aromas).

Precise: Often used when describing how a wine feels in the mouth; it is almost always tied to its acidity. You might also see the terms "linear" or "focused" used. It means that the wine's texture travels almost in a straight line down the tongue.

Pure: If a wine's flavors and/or aromas evoke specific fruits, herbs, or other notes, we often use the term "pure" or mention "purity." This means that if a wine smells like fresh strawberries, for example, then it *really* smells *exactly* like fresh strawberries.

Sexy: Describes a wine that presents in a showy, obvious way, and/or has fruit flavors and body that feel generous and luxurious in the mouth. This can often be because the wine is both very fruity and very powerful in body and alcohol.

Spicy: A wine that has aromas and/or flavors of spices. These are usually related to baking spices (such as cinnamon, cardamom, nutmeg, or cloves) but can also be used to describe both fresh and dried herbs (like thyme, mint, or tea leaves).

1. LOOK

We live in an amazing time for wine lovers, perhaps the best time ever. Global competition, combined with an explosion of tastemaker opinions online and through social media, has created a market in which wine producers really have to deliver the goods in order to sell anything. The last three decades have seen dramatic rises in both the diversity and quality of wine, more so than at any other point in human history. And it's all available at lower relative price points than ever before, too. Ironically, this makes the first tasting step—looking—less important (but more fun!) than it has ever been.

It used to be that looking at a wine in the glass helped identify winemaking faults or storage issues. For example, wines with odd, noticeable cloudiness could signal a chemical issue during winemaking, or a wine that might be spoiling would show telltale color changes. These days, you are unlikely to encounter such faults.

While such a visual inspection is now less necessary, there are still plenty of reasons to look at the wine in your glass before putting it into your mouth. For one, wine has some of the most beautiful hues of any beverage. The spectrum of rosé wines alone can range from the most elegant, gray-tinged pink to a sexy salmon and even to a deep blood red. Personally, I find looking at wine in the glass akin to staring at gemstones: it's worth a minute or two just to appreciate how downright *gorgeous* it can be. Skipping it would be like diving into a perfectly plated gourmet meal without looking at the care and detail that went into its presentation.

Apart from slowing you down a bit and getting your mind ready for your first sip, looking at the wine in the glass can provide other clues. White wines tend to gain color as they age, with darker, honeyed hues. The opposite is true for red wines, which lose color over time (you might hear the term "precipitate" used to describe this) and will show orange "bricking" (starting at the edges and moving inward). The depth of colors can also provide a hint to your mouth of what's to come. (Richer wines, and those aged in wood, tend to have deeper shades.) Observing a glass of wine against a white background, with good light behind you, will help with this step (though it's certainly not required).

Much fuss has been made over the years about a wine's "legs" (the rivulets of wine that adhere to the sides of the glass after swirling), but in my experience these tell you less about a wine's body and more about its viscosity, and are usually just a fun and pretty aspect to admire without drawing conclusions.

Finally, note how much wine is in your glass; you want it to be about one-third full, covering just up to the largest width of the glass's bowl. Otherwise, when we get to the next step, you (or the poor unsuspecting folks in your immediate vicinity) might be wearing the wine, rather than tasting it.

Wine has some of the most diverse and beautiful hues of any beverage.

2. SWIRL

Your next step is to swirl the wine in the glass. In my experience, this step seems to trip people up the most, as they try to mimic a "perfect" swirl and instead end up creating a larger dry-cleaning bill. My professional advice to you: there is no perfect swirl, so do what comes naturally and don't worry about how it looks (just keep it in the glass).

I prefer to swirl with the foot of the glass on a table, moving counter-clockwise (there's no preference on direction, by the way). Occasionally, I'll swirl while standing but I find that this has a higher percentage chance of getting wine on my shoes, because I'm clumsy. This is why it's important not to attempt a swirl with an overfilled glass. (It's better to dump, or drink, the excess first.)

To perform the swirl, simply hold the glass in one hand and move your hand in repeated, short circles until the wine begins to create a sort of small whirlpool in your glass. It only takes a moment or two, but getting the wine some air is crucial. You want to expose as much of the wine's surface area to air as possible, and swirling is the best way to do that. This is essential for releasing the volatile compounds that are largely responsible for how the wine tastes. Skip this step and you run the risk of the wine tasting flat and boring.

This step has a side benefit; namely that you can cup your hand on the bowl of the glass and get a sense for whether or not the wine is at the right temperature. If a red wine is too cold, for example, it will taste overly dull. You can warm it up by simply holding the bowl of the glass in the palm of your hand for a while. It also gives you another chance to see the wine's various hues.

KEEPING A WINE JOURNAL

To further develop your wine-tasting palate and taste memory, consider keeping (or buying) a wine journal, and recording your evaluation of each new wine that you drink. Many options exist for this, including phone apps that allow you to annotate your tasting and can pull in relevant details using only a photo of the wine's label.

A good wine journal should note the producer, vintage, name, and region of the wine and should include ample space for you to note details about the color, aromas, flavors, and overall tasting impressions of each wine. If you find that you're still building up your tasting vocabulary, there are journals available that include lists of aroma and tasting descriptors from which you can choose, which helps you capture your tasting experience more quickly (and gets you focusing on your personal notes and impressions faster, too).

---

3. SMELL

This is the most important step in the tasting process, and wine simply cannot be properly enjoyed without it. How you smell is up to you, but unlike spirits or harder drinks, almost all wines are best smelled with your nose right on the edge of the glass's rim. Just hold the glass up and take a sniff. You want to get all of those volatile aromatic compounds that you so dutifully released during the swirl into your nasal cavity, so that your brain can start to process the wine's aromas.

How long you should sniff depends on what you have in your glass. Some wines aren't that complex and will offer less to contemplate. Others will be "quiet" and require more sniffing to appreciate. Some will almost scream at you, with aromas jumping out of the glass. High-end wines will change over time as they warm in the glass, rewarding multiple sniffs to note how the aromas are evolving.

When it comes to this step, you can learn a lot from how man's best friend sniffs. Ever try to pull a dog away when smelling something it finds interesting? It's not easy. That's because dogs are intensely focused on the data that their noses are collecting. Mimicking that kind of focus when smelling a wine will reward you with more aromatic details. Varying your sniffs, much like a dog does (between long/slow sniffs, and deep/short sniffs), also helps pick up different intensities of aromas.

From time to time, try concentrating the wine's aromas by covering the mouth of the glass with one hand, while swirling the wine with the other and then lifting your hand away and taking another sniff. The point is to get all of the aromatic details that the wine has to offer. It's like any food—the more you can get out of it, the more you can appreciate and contemplate.

4. TASTE

It sounds counterintuitive, but the actual tasting portion is often the quickest of the entire tasting process. Take a sip, gently swirling the wine around in your mouth, allowing it to coat your palate, gums, and tongue. This reveals the texture of the wine, its impressions of intensity, body, volume, weight, and alcoholic power. It also releases additional volatile compounds, further enhancing the flavors and aromas.

Critical evaluations require quite a bit of swirling around, but for most purposes a quick swirl will do. You'll likely find that after swirling once or twice, you can continue enjoying the wine just fine (after all, it's not mouthwash). All the while, you'll want to consider how the wine feels in your mouth. What do you notice about it? What flavors does it evoke? Are the perceptions of acidity, bitterness, and power in balance, or do some stand out over others? This is the most brain-intensive part of the process, because there's an almost palpable switch between the more emotional reactions our brains have during sniffing, to engaging our conscious brain to interpret what we are tasting.

THE SLURPY SIP: REALLY NECESSARY?

Wine pros are famous (okay, *infamous*) for the Slurpy Sip. This is when, directly after putting a sip of wine into their mouths, they suck in a bit of air before swallowing (or spitting) the wine. This results in a slurping, gurgling sound that, while not exactly unpleasant, isn't what you want to hear at the dinner table, either.

Is this Slurpy Sip really necessary? If you're trying to get a handle on a wine, then yeah, you'll want to do it. What this does is expose the wine to more air while in your mouth, releasing more volatile compounds than would be freed just by drinking it. These compounds are then tasted retronasally (through the back of your mouth, after interacting with your tongue), revealing more aromas and flavors. The Slurpy Sip is best avoided at, say, a family gathering or a fancy dinner, but is helpful to do on your own (and often essential when reviewing a wine professionally).

5. CONSIDER

After the first four steps, you can either spit the wine out into a cup or sink (if you plan on tasting many wines, this is essential to avoid getting snockered) or (more likely) swallow the wine and notice how it interacts with your palate on the way down.

A key aspect of wine, and one that makes it so enthralling, is what we call the finish. This is shorthand for what lingers in your mouth (and for how long) after sipping a wine. Higher quality wines tend to have a long, complex finish that evokes the aromas and flavors from the previous steps. Lower quality wines will have shorter finishes. Some wines actually have intense, long finishes that you might find unpleasant. Your mileage, as they say, will vary!

Note your impressions on the wine, good or bad, as soon as possible. There are several reasons for this but the primary benefit is immediacy: you're unlikely to recall a wine's details later (especially after several sips or multiple wines). Trust me, I do this for a living and even I get tripped up on my recollection after the fact. The more quickly you can note your impressions, focusing on what you really enjoyed (so that you can repeat the experience) or really disliked (so that you can avoid it), the better. Journaling your tasting will also help reinforce your memory about the wine and provide a handy reference later.

A Beginner's Tasting

Not sure where to start? Here's a tasting to get the beginners among you started, highlighting easy-to-drink wines with quickly identifiable characteristics. Consider this a palate calibration.

Korbel Brut Sparkling Wine (California)

Korbel's multi-variety blends are everything that a budget sparkling wine should be. Crisp, clean, and refreshing on the palate, with apple flavors and citrus and baked bread on the nose, this pale gold sparkler is the perfect precursor for what you should expect from well-made sparkling wine.

Pacific Rim Riesling (Columbia Valley, Washington)

This white is a downright killer with Chinese takeout. Pale gold and bursting with honeysuckle and mandarin orange aromas, the palate is light but has a sense of roundness from its off-dry style. Apple, pear, and lemon-drop flavors are staples of this wine, all coming from the grape itself, making it a good ambassador for Riesling in general.

Black Box Sauvignon Blanc (Chile)

Yes, this comes in a box (technically, a bag within a box). Sourced from vineyards throughout Chile, this light yellow wine has a medium body, zesty acidity, and citrus flavors, along with Sauvignon Blanc's signature herbal, grassy aromas. An added bonus: you'll have plenty left over to serve guests.

Dark Horse Rosé (California)

A light pink salmon color is what greets you when you pour this wine . . . out of its can. Canned wines are no joke, as this rosé shows in its ample floral aromas, refreshing body, and red berry flavors. It's a good way to get introduced to the dry rosé style without your bank account even breaking a sweat.

La Posta Pizzella Malbec (Mendoza, Argentina)

This deep-violet-hued wine is sourced from a single, high-elevation Argentine vineyard, and it's a nice pick for discovering both the grape and the region. Not only do you get textbook Malbec aspects (like black cherry, licorice, and tobacco notes, plummy flavors, and full body), you also get nice hints of vanilla and cedar from oak aging.

CHAPTER 2

THE GRAPE VARIETIES

To understand why wines taste (and smell) the way that they do, you have to start with their main ingredient: grapes. At the end of the day (well, technically, the growing season), it's the grape variety that provides the bedrock of flavor, aroma, texture, and structure upon which everything else in a wine is built.

In this chapter, you'll get introduced to the most famous (and some not-so-famous) wine grape varieties, with a focus on what it is about each of them that imparts those wildly varied primary tastes and smells to their resulting wines.

How Grapes Grow

All grape varieties go through the same growing process. They send out shoots, then bud and flower. Grapes then develop and grow for about 100 days, during which they change color (called *veraison*), ripen, and finally are harvested. The devil's in the details, though, and each variety prefers a different combination of factors to achieve grape ripeness. Those factors can be summed up in the old real estate adage, "location, location, location!" Certain growing areas sport the right combination of temperatures, soil types, sun exposure, weather, and other variables that make some grape varieties more successful in those spots than others.

TERROIR

Wines from much of Western Europe list a place name rather than a grape variety on their labels. While there are regulations behind that (such as which grapes can be used, which vinification techniques are permitted, how long they must be aged, etc.), traditionally this developed from the concept of *terroir*—a French term encompassing all of the unique aspects that go into growing grapes and making wine from a particular place. *Terroir* is why the same clone of Riesling planted in the Mosel, in Austria, and in the Finger Lakes, vinified in the same way, will produce wines that are distinctly different from one another.

Grapes are a bit like Goldilocks: they want everything to be *juuuuust riiiiight*; and "just right" is different for each variety. The right combinations of rootstock, soil type and nutrients, sunlight, heat, moisture, pruning (which happens year-round), ventilation, and wind exposure all differ among wine grape varieties. The more care taken in matching those factors to the variety, the better the chances of making more flavorful wines from the resulting harvest.

Here are just a few of the growing-factor landmines that await modern wine grape farmers:

How Growing Conditions Can Affect Grapes

GROWING FACTOR	TOO LITTLE	TOO MUCH
Vine vigor	Limits vine productivity	Vine spends too much energy on its leaves, and not enough on its grapes
Grape yield	Usually concentrated berries, just not enough of them	Too many underdeveloped grapes, lacking complexity and flavor
Sunlight (this includes sun exposure, and the degree to which the grapes are shielded from the sun by their leaves)	Underripe grapes with overly "green" flavors and aromas	Overripe or sunburned grapes that have prune, raisin, or other off-flavors
Moisture (including rainfall and soil drainage)	Dried-out grapes, lower production	Increased disease pressure on the vines, rot on the grapes, and/or watered-down grape flavors
Soil nutrients	Diminished vine health	Potentially unremarkable, generic-tasting wine
Wind	Increased disease and rot	Interference with flowering, lowering production
Heat	Potentially underripe grapes, prolonged ripening season	Overripe grapes with potentially excessive alcohol

In general, European wine areas (or "Old World" wine regions with many decades of historical precedent) have strict legal regulations governing the *when*, *how*, and *how much* when it comes to growing and harvesting wine grapes. These all impact the flavor profile of the wines from those regions, which are expected to conform to certain standards in order to carry a regional designation on the label. "New World" regions, like Chile and the United States, have fewer such restrictions, though these tend to increase as you narrow down geographically, with single-vineyard wines facing the strictest regulations.

In all cases, the trick with growing wine grapes is to maximize the potential for the flavors, body, and aromas for which the producer is aiming. The goal is almost always achieving the right amount of ripeness, a balance of sweetness and acidity. That perfect degree of ripeness is harder to reach in cooler regions, and easier to overshoot in hotter ones. Older wine regions simply have had more time to figure this all out through trial and error, and they've combined that hard-earned knowledge into the concept of *terroir*.

Harvested grapes being prepared for transport to the winery

WEATHER

Weather is, after sunlight, the most important factor in growing wine grapes to proper ripeness. Excessively warm weather will potentially over-ripen grapes (if not dry out some grapes entirely), causing prune-like or dried fruit flavors. Excessively cool spells can show "greener" or underripe flavors and aromas. Very wet weather can cause disease, mildew, and rot, and limit harvests (or produce watered-down flavors). Severe weather, such as extreme wind or hail, can significantly reduce (or entirely wipe out) grape yields.

Wines blended from grapes grown across very large areas will have fewer quality and flavor impacts from weather variances vintage to vintage. That's because there are more grapes and growing conditions from which to source those wines (think "California" or "southeastern Australia"). The more specific the place designation (such as "Rutherford" in Napa Valley), the more unique and distinctive the wine can be, but the impact the weather can have on quality, flavor, and aroma in each vintage will be larger. Average weather patterns are the primary reason why specific grape varieties thrive when planted in certain areas, at various elevations, and with certain directional exposures.

WHEN THE GRAPES ARE HARVESTED

Different grape varieties will ripen at different times, and sometimes the threat of rain or other inclement weather can force a grape farmer's hand when it comes to the timing of harvest. The picking time has a direct impact on a wine's eventual flavor characteristics.

Generally, grapes are harvested from August to October in the Northern Hemisphere and February to April in the Southern Hemisphere (global warming is beginning to shift those times earlier in many regions). Grapes meant for sparkling wine, white wine, and rosé wines are usually harvested on the earlier end of that spectrum, with red wine grapes being harvested later. Style comes into play here, too; some producers might intentionally harvest early (to preserve acidity), or later (to maximize body and ripeness). Grapes harvested earlier will show greener, more herbal characteristics, with lighter body potential and more acidity. Harvesting on the later side (giving the grapes more "hang time") will provide less acidity but more potential alcohol and riper fruit flavors. It's common for multiple pickings to happen, even for the same grape variety, so that the differing flavor results can be blended together into the final wine.

Sorry to kill the romance, but you should know that the vast majority of wine grapes are harvested mechanically; this is much faster (and cheaper) than harvesting by hand but is rougher on the grapes. Premium wines tend to require more expensive hand-harvesting (for gentler treatment of the fruit, and greater care in selecting the best berries). Some wines, such as certain dessert wines like Sauternes (see The Wonder of the Noble Rot, page 24) and Icewine (made from grapes allowed to freeze on the vine, which concentrates their sugars), require several rounds of difficult, expensive hand-harvesting (which you pay for in the purchase price).

Icewine is created from ripe grapes that freeze while still on the vine, concentrating their sugars.

THE WONDER OF THE NOBLE ROT

If you've ever wondered who first saw a lobster and thought, "I don't care what that oversized bug looks like, I'm eating it," you'll appreciate the dessert wine phenomenon known as "noble rot."

Noble rot is the product of a gray fungus, *Botrytis cinerea*, that affects ripened wine grapes, usually those planted near sources of moisture (like rivers), but that also experience some periods of drier weather. While it looks entirely unappetizing, botrytis's impact on ripe and overripe grapes can be amazing, concentrating their acids and sugars, and turning what juice remains in each berry into an incredible nectar.

"Noble rot" may not look appealing, but it creates some of the world's greatest dessert wines.

The resulting wines are vibrant and syrupy, with luscious texture, lower alcohol, and ultra-pure fruit flavors. They almost always have intense aromas, with notes of brioche and yeast imparted by the fungus. These wines are said to be "botrytized." Grape yields for botrytized wines can be incredibly low, and require manual harvesting and more winemaking care and labor. For those reasons, they can be expensive and are among the most coveted of all dessert wines. Examples include France's Sauternes, Hungary's Tokai Aszú, and some dessert Riesling and Gewürztraminer wines from Germany and other countries.

GOING GREEN: ORGANIC AND BIODYNAMIC FARMING

While we all like to envision a wine grape farmer stepping out from his porch in the early morning mist, lovingly tending to the grapes growing in perfectly manicured rows in his backyard, the reality is that precious few wine grapes are farmed that way. Just as we don't expect a fast-food sandwich to be made with the finest ingredients, we shouldn't be surprised that budget wine grapes are farmed conventionally (which means permitting the use of pesticides, insecticides, and the like). This doesn't mean that budget wines are terrible, but it does mean that the less expensive a wine is, generally the less health conscious and delicate its farming practices.

Recent decades have seen a significant shift in the wine world toward sustainable, organic, and biodynamic farming. Sustainability is seldom regulated, though some wine regions are banding together to create guidelines that can be adopted by multiple producers and even other countries. California's Lodi Rules for Sustainable Winegrowing is one such program; the regulations for organic farming differ from country to country, but for grapes to be "Certified Green" by Lodi Rules, the grower must not use chemical fertilizers, fungicides, herbicides, and pesticides. For a wine to carry the Lodi Rules seal, it must contain 85 percent "Certified Green" grapes.

Another step—and a topic that can induce fistfights among wine geeks—is implementing biodynamics, a method of agriculture based on the ideas of Austrian philosopher Rudolf Steiner in the early 20th century. Steiner was eccentric (some say nuts), and a few biodynamic farming practices might strike the layperson as odd (these include planting according to lunar phases and planetary cycles). There is, however, a growing body of evidence showing that some of those practices make scientific sense, providing natural solutions to several farming challenges.

Both mediocre and great wines can be made from grapes farmed conventionally, organically, or biodynamically; some just might be healthier to imbibe than others. If anything, greener practices at least get wine producers more involved with care in the vineyard, which almost always translates to making better wine.

The Varieties

Following are the grape varieties you're most likely to encounter on today's wine labels. This is by no means a comprehensive list of the grapes used to make wine; that topic is squarely outside the scope of this book (there are hundreds of varieties indigenous to Italy alone).

BARBERA

bar/BEH/rah

Barbera is a star of northern Italy's Piedmont region, where it probably originated (references to the variety in Piedmont's Monferrato area date back to the 13th century). Wines from this red grape are ruby in color with a pink rim, medium-bodied, and robustly fruity, with aromas and flavors of red berries, cherries, and plums. It almost always has lighter tannins and bouncy acidity, making it food-friendly. It's quite versatile, too, found in fresh, fruity styles as well as more elegant versions (as in Asti) and even age-worthy, powerful, oak-aged wines (as in Alba).

While Piedmont is its home and offers the most delectable examples of its wines, Barbera takes well to different soil types and climates and has become quite a world traveler. (Amador County, in California, has an annual festival devoted entirely to Barbera.)

Range of possible flavors: Raspberry, blueberry, dark cherry, plum

Wines that use this grape: Barbera d'Alba, Barbera d'Asti

Major production areas: Argentina, Italy (Alba, Asti), United States (California)

IF YOU LIKE THIS, TRY: *Pinot Noir, Sangiovese, Zinfandel*

CABERNET FRANC

ka/behr/NAY FRAHN

Medium-bodied and garnet in the glass, Cabernet Franc is often confused with Cabernet Sauvignon, one of the varieties it is blended with in famous Bordeaux reds. Generally, it has similar flavors but a lighter color and lower acidity (but just as much richness) than Cabernet Sauvignon. Its highlight feature is its intense herbal spiciness: it can offer a nose full of dried and fresh herbs, bell pepper, tobacco leaves, and violets.

The cooler the growing area (such as along the Loire River in France), the more pronounced its herbal spices can be; the warmer and sunnier the region (such as Napa Valley), the more Cabernet Franc will do its best Cabernet Sauvignon impression, with darker spices and riper fruit flavors.

Range of possible flavors: Black currant, raspberry, tobacco, dried and fresh herbs, spices, violet

Wines that use this grape: Bordeaux, Chinon

Major production areas: Argentina, Canada, France (Bordeaux, Loire Valley), Italy, United States (California)

IF YOU LIKE THIS, TRY: *Cabernet Sauvignon, Carménère, Merlot*

CABERNET SAUVIGNON

ka/behr/NAY soh/vee/NYAWN

Cabernet Sauvignon is the world's most recognizable red wine grape variety. It's easier to list the regions that *don't* grow it than those that do, and it's *the* key component of the most celebrated red wines of Bordeaux, Napa Valley, and many other regions. Cabernet's status as the red grape king is remarkable, in that it has only existed for a handful of centuries. (That's not long, in wine history terms.) DNA evidence shows that Cabernet Sauvignon is likely from Bordeaux, as it's a cross of Cabernet Franc and Sauvignon Blanc, both native to that area.

Cabernet Sauvignon, the world's most famous red grape variety

Part of Cabernet's incredible popularity can be attributed to how well it adapts to different climates and soils. Cooler climates emphasize Cabernet's red fruit side and show its herbal and spice notes; warmer climes move its flavors to darker fruits, with drier herb and jammier aromas. Cabernet's ability to create everything from simple, entry-level reds to show-stopping, complex beasts that can age for decades in the bottle plays no small part in securing its position as one of wine's most famous grape names.

You can count on some things from almost all Cabernet Sauvignon wines: fuller body, medium acidity, and a garnet hue that moves to brick-red as it ages.

Range of possible flavors: Red and black currant, plum, herbs, baking spices, cedar, tomato leaf, tobacco, graphite, truffle, mint, eucalyptus

Wines that use this grape: Bolgheri, Bordeaux, Meritage red blends (United States)

Major production areas: Argentina, Australia (Barossa Valley, Coonawarra, Margaret River), Canada, Chile (Maipo Valley), France (Bordeaux), Israel, Italy (Bolgheri), Spain (Navarra, Ribera del Duero, Somontano), United States (Napa Valley, Paso Robles, Sonoma County, Washington State)

IF YOU LIKE THIS, TRY: *Cabernet Franc, Merlot, Petit Verdot*

CARIGNAN

KAR/in/yan

Known by several names (including Cariñena, Mazuelo, Samsó), this Spanish red grape is ancient, and became popular among growers for its ability to produce high grape yields. This traditionally made Carignan a blending component in everything from bulk jug wines to higher-end, bold red blends.

Despite its deep red color, bold tannins, and raging acidity, Carignan's flavors can be mild and tangy, trending toward red fruits. Its spiciness can be lovely, and when its yields are held in check it adds depth, complexity, and structure (especially to Spanish red blends). While rare, varietal Carignan wines can be highly aromatic, enticing, and long-lived in the bottle (thanks to all of that tannin and acidity).

Range of possible flavors: Raspberry, red plum, dried cranberry, red and black licorice, baking spices, bacon

Wines that use this grape: Red blends in France (Corbières, Fitou, Minervois) and Spain (Montsant, Penedès, Priorat, Rioja)

Major production areas: Chile, France (Languedoc-Roussillon), Italy (Sardinia), Morocco, Spain, Tunisia, United States (California's Central Valley)

IF YOU LIKE THIS, TRY: *Grenache/Garnacha, Monastrell/Mourvèdre, Syrah/Shiraz*

CARMÉNÈRE

kahr/mhen/NEHRE

Carménère is native to France's Médoc area in Bordeaux and was once thought extinct (after much of Europe's vineyards were devastated by the phylloxera louse plague of 1867). Intrepid growers from Chile, however, had imported Carménère cuttings from France in the 19th century, planting it widely in an attempt to mimic the red wine blends of Bordeaux. For several decades, they believed Carménère to be Merlot, thus inadvertently rescuing the variety from destruction.

Today, Carménère can be found in many varietal and blended red wines from Chile. Although its name comes from the French word for crimson (*carmin*), that refers to the color of its leaves in autumn, not to the deep red color of its wines. Carménère is notable for its combination of medium to full body and low tannins, making it relatively easy to drink. It has ample spiciness on the nose, ranging from smoke and leather notes to dark tobacco, and is somewhat notorious for being susceptible to methoxypyrazines, which can create a love-it-or-hate-it green bell pepper/jalapeño aroma.

Range of possible flavors: Red fruits, cherry, leather, smoke, spices, tobacco, bell pepper, herbs

Wines that use this grape: Chilean reds, some Bordeaux-style red blends

Major production area: Chile

IF YOU LIKE THIS, TRY: *Cabernet Franc*

CHARDONNAY

shar/doh/NAY

Chardonnay, the queen of white wine grapes, is the most widely planted and most popular variety in the world. Native to France's Burgundy, it prefers chalky soils (such as in Champagne) but is so adaptable that it is grown (or, at least, has been attempted) in just about every wine region globally. It's probably been with us for a long time: Chardonnay is a cross between Pinot Noir and the ancient Gouais Blanc, and evidence suggests that it was cultivated in Burgundy since Roman times.

The queen of white wine grapes: Chardonnay

While often criticized for being a bit neutral in flavor while heavier in palate weight, Chardonnay's versatility is impressive and is one of its greatest assets. In cooler regions (like Burgundy's Chablis), it produces pale gold, medium-bodied floral wines with apple flavors and enough acidity to be made into sparkling wine. (It's the major component of the best bubbles from Champagne, Italy's Franciacorta, and Crémant wines throughout France.) In warmer areas (such as Napa Valley), it ripens to produce full-bodied, rich, dark gold wines with tropical fruit flavors; these are often aged in oak, where they take on creamy, toasty notes with hints of coconut and additional palate depth. If you think that you don't like Chardonnay, chances are good that you just haven't found the *right* Chardonnay style for you . . . *yet*.

Range of possible flavors: Apple, pear, tropical fruits, white blossoms, vanilla, cream, toast, butter

Wines that use this grape: Blanc de Blancs, Chablis, Champagne, Côte d'Or, Crémant, Franciacorta, Mâcon, Trento DOC; many sparkling, varietal, and late harvest dessert wines

Major production areas: Argentina, Australia, Canada, France (Burgundy, Champagne), Chile, Italy, New Zealand, South Africa, Spain, United States (California—notably Napa Valley, New York, Oregon, Washington State)

IF YOU LIKE THIS, TRY: *Chenin Blanc, Pinot Blanc, Viognier*

CHENIN BLANC

SHUN/ihn BLAHN

Many grape varieties are said to be versatile. Chenin Blanc laughs at most of those varieties. Native to France's Loire Valley, Chenin Blanc might be the *most* versatile white wine grape. It can be made into sparkling wine (thanks to its medium to high acid levels), or dry white wines in multiple styles (from fresh and simple to oaky and complex), and even off-dry and dessert wines. And all of those are *just* in the Loire!

In its simpler forms, Chenin tends toward apple and quince flavors, with melon and mandarin notes (and spicy, floral aromas) coming in more complex, age-worthy versions. Its color changes in chameleon-like fashion, too, from shades of straw (in dry wines) to amber gold (in sweeter versions). Growing Chenin since the 1600s, South Africa has staked a claim as the grape's "New World" wine home (where it's also known as "Steen").

Range of possible flavors: Apple, quince, melon, mandarin orange, verbena, jasmine, straw, lanolin

Wines that use this grape: Anjou, Crémant de Loire, Vouvray, and varietal wines from California and South Africa

Major production areas: Australia, France (Loire Valley), South Africa, United States (California)

IF YOU LIKE THIS, TRY: *Chardonnay, Viognier*

GAMAY

gam/MAY

Gamay, or Gamay Noir, is an ancient variety from France's Burgundy that is most famous for being *infamous*. Its earliest reference is from July 1395, when it was named a "very bad and disloyal variety" by Duc Philippe le Hardi in Dijon, and banned for being "harmful to human creatures."

Gamay: the grape behind the vibrant red wines of Beaujolais.

Thankfully, Gamay is recovering from this royal blow to its reputation. It's best known for producing the fruity, floral, grape-bubblegum guilty pleasure of Beaujolais Nouveau, a light red wine that's released in November immediately after harvest. There's more to Gamay, however, particularly when it's crafted from one of the exceptional ten *Cru* vineyards north of Lyon (Brouilly, Chénas, Chiroubles, Côte de Brouilly, Fleurie, Juliénas, Morgon, Moulin-à-Vent, Régnié, and Saint-Amour).

Generally, Gamay wine is light purple in color, light in body and tannins (and irresistibly easy to drink), and big on acidity (making it a great all-around Thanksgiving dinner pairing). In its simplest forms, banana, violet, and red berry aromas combine with intense, direct red fruit flavors for an easy, gulpable wine. *Cru* Beaujolais Gamay, however, shows depth, complexity, peppery spice, and darker red fruit flavors, all without sacrificing Gamay's signature drinkability and freshness. In my experience (I'm a total *Cru* Beaujolais fanboy), aged Gamay wines from those areas are some of the most underrated reds in the world. (For a primer, check out the Gamay tasting on page 34.)

Range of possible flavors: Red berries, plum, banana, grape, bubblegum, black/white pepper, violet

Wines that use this grape: Beaujolais

Major production areas: England, France (Beaujolais), Germany, Switzerland

IF YOU LIKE THIS, TRY: *Blaufränkisch, Brachetto, Tavel Rosé*

Gamay Beyond Nouveau

There's (much) more to Gamay than guzzling uber-fruity Beaujolais Nouveau. Here are examples of how Gamay can strut its stuff, all from France's Beaujolais region. Try them and you might just find your new favorite red wine jam.

Louis Jadot Beaujolais

Tangy, fruity, and light reddish-purple in the glass, Jadot's Gamay is all raspberry fruitiness and jumping acidity. This step up from Beaujolais Nouveau will give you a great sense of how Gamay can be approachable but still have a bit of a serious side.

Drouhin Beaujolais Villages

This region consists of 38 villages in the north of Beaujolais, with the Gamay vines grown on better soils. The result in the glass is more: more light purple color and more complexity. That starts with aromas of violets and pepper and black raspberry flavors and ends with a light body that refreshes even when slightly chilled.

Georges Duboeuf Clos des Quatres Vents Fleurie

As its name implies (it translates to "flower"), wines from this Cru are often floral and almost always pretty. The color is darker purple, and the aromas are more intense (with violets, blackberries, and earth). It's lovely drinking, but also structured enough to stand up to chicken or pork dishes.

Domaine des Maisons Neuves Les Bois-Combes Moulin-à-Vent

Moulin-à-Vent is considered the King of Gamay and the most age-worthy of the Beaujolais Crus. Reddish-purple in the glass, this has more body and more tannic structure than you'd expect from Gamay, with black cherry flavors and pepper, perfume, and dark berry aromas. Delicious right away, it will also age wonderfully, eventually rewarding the patient with spicier, earthier aromas and tangy plum flavors.

Domaine Marcel Lapierre Morgon

Morgon is known for the juiciest, jammiest expression of Gamay, and that's exactly what you get with this brilliantly purple wine. Raspberry and peppery spice aromas are matched with a beautifully round, medium-bodied palate that feels fresh and focused to the last drop.

GEWÜRZTRAMINER

guh/VURTS/trah/mee/ner

Difficult to say, but easy to love, dark-golden Gewürztraminer wines are among the most aromatic whites you'll find. Its name means "Spicy Traminer," and it is best known for having intense smells of rose petals, tropical fruits, and lychee nuts. It tends to produce fuller-bodied, lower-acid wines, developing enough natural sugars to make it shine in off-dry styles. In its native Alsace, it is the main variety in some of the region's most coveted wines. A versatile grape, Gewürztraminer is made into dry, off-dry, sweet, and even "noble rot" dessert versions. (See The Wonder of the Noble Rot on page 24 for more on this.)

While a white wine grape, Gewürztraminer berries develop pinkish-red skins.

For the most part, cooler climates are a must for this variety, whose pink-skinned grapes are a bit fussy when it comes to weather and soil types. Cooler regions allow Gewürztraminer to fully ripen without getting out of hand in terms of potential alcohol. Gewürztraminer's natural spiciness and residual sugar both make it a fantastic pairing for spicier foods (try it with Indian cuisine for an unforgettable match).

Range of possible flavors: Citrus, apricot, tropical fruits, peach, lychee nut, ginger, allspice, rose petal, toast, smoke

Wines that use this grape: Alsace Grand Cru, varietal wines from California, France, Germany, and Italy

Major production areas: Australia (Clare Valley), France (Alsace), Germany, Hungary, Italy (Trentino-Alto Adige), New Zealand, United States (California, Washington State)

IF YOU LIKE THIS, TRY: *Moscato, Sémillon*

GRENACHE/GARNACHA

gruh/NAHSH (gar/NAT/ja)

It often surprises wine lovers to learn that Grenache (or Garnacha in Spain)—low in acid, tannin, and color—is one of the most widely planted wine grapes in the world. A key component of many full-bodied reds, it's found in wines from France, Spain, California, and the Italian islands. It builds lots of potential alcohol as it ripens over a long period, preferring sunny and warm climates, and is prone to oxidizing (so even its younger wines tend to show some orange edges around its bright, transparent ruby core).

Grenache usually needs some help from other grapes to produce wine with enough structure for aging, and it excels as a blending component (hence its popularity). Great stand-alone Grenache wines can also be made, and their combination of peppery, floral, and fruity aromas and strong body can be (literally and figuratively) intoxicating in their deliciousness.

Range of possible flavors: Raspberry (red and black), strawberry, white pepper, violet, coffee, leather

Wines that use this grape: Châteauneuf-du-Pape, Côtes du Rhône, Priorat, Rioja, Tavel

Major production areas: Australia (McLaren Vale), France (Châteauneuf-du-Pape, Côtes du Rhône, Tavel), Italy (Sardinia, Sicily), Spain (Calatayud, Cariñena, Priorat), United States (California, including Monterey, Santa Barbara)

IF YOU LIKE THIS, TRY: *Monastrell/Mourvèdre, Syrah/Shiraz*

GRÜNER VELTLINER

grew/ner velt/LEE/ner

Grüner Veltliner dates back to Roman times and is now the darling white wine grape of Austria. It's versatile—Grüner can be found in everything from jug wines to entry-level sippers to premium single-vineyard wines—and surprising (often combining vibrant acidity, ripe citrus, and stone fruit flavors with an excitingly unexpected blend of vegetal and spice aromas).

Grüner's jaunty, lighter-to-medium-bodied palate, lemon color, and one-two fruit/herbal combo punch all make it perfect to pair with salad courses. While you can enjoy the refreshing qualities of a young Grüner Veltliner wine immediately, premium versions take on lovely honey, toast, nut, and dried white fig elements as they age.

Range of possible flavors: Stone fruits, citrus, white pepper, celery, herbs, lentils

Wines that use this grape: Varietal wines, also Austrian Sekt (sparkling)

Major production areas: Australia (Adelaide Hills), Austria (Kremstal, Niederösterreich, Wachau), Czech Republic, Germany, Hungary, Italy (Trentino-Alto Adige), United States (California, New York State Finger Lakes)

IF YOU LIKE THIS, TRY: *Riesling, Sauvignon Blanc*

MALBEC

MAHL/behk

Malbec is most closely associated with Argentina, but its home is France: it's one of the six grape varieties permitted in Bordeaux red blends and is the grape found in the red wines of Cahors. Few would argue, however, that Malbec doesn't love the warm, dry conditions of Argentina's high-altitude vineyards.

Though French in origin, Malbec has achieved new heights in Argentina.

Inky violet in color, almost always full-bodied, somewhat tannic, and sporting juicy fruitiness and strong tobacco aromas, Malbec is a hefty sipper and a natural match for steak (which might help explain why it fits so well in South America). In cooler areas like Cahors, Malbec shows more dried herb characteristics and redder plum flavors. Sunnier spots like Argentina's Mendoza bring out Malbec's muscular side, with dominant blackberry flavors, a juicy palate, and plenty of power.

Range of possible flavors: Blackberry, red plum, tobacco, dark cocoa, vanilla

Wines that use this grape: Cahors, Libournais, varietal wines from Argentina and California

Major production areas: Argentina (Mendoza), Chile (Central Valley), France (Cahors), United States (California, Washington State)

IF YOU LIKE THIS, TRY: *Merlot, Petit Verdot, Petite Sirah*

MERLOT

mehr/LOH

Though maligned as the vinous villain of the novel and movie *Sideways*, Merlot remains one of the most noble and notable red wine grapes. It is one of the main blending grapes of Bordeaux (where it likely originated), and is the primary grape of the Pomerol area's expensive and exclusive wines. Merlot also plays an important role in some of the most prestigious wine regions in the United States, especially Napa Valley.

Merlot is a key component of many of Bordeaux's most coveted wines.

Merlot is almost always dark blue in the glass, is soft and round in the mouth, and leans toward a fuller-bodied palate. It ranges in style from easy-drinking, plummy wines with little tannins to more burly, long-lived wines that are blacker in fruit and closer in spirit to Cabernet Sauvignon. Merlot offers juicy, plump fruit flavors and often a distinctive aromatic note of olives.

Thankfully, Merlot is recovering from the consumer backlash it recently suffered, and many excellent renditions can be found worldwide. If you enjoy suppleness, softness, and body in your reds, Merlot ought to be your first stop on your wine journey. (You can get started with the tasting on page 40.)

Range of possible flavors: Plum, boysenberry, blackberry, blueberry, cassis, olive, leather, mushroom, herbs

Wines that use this grape: Bergerac, Bordeaux (Bordeaux Supérieur, Graves, Médoc, Pomerol, Saint-Émilion, Saint-Estèphe), Languedoc-Roussillon, varietal wines from Argentina, California, Chile, Washington

Major production areas: Argentina (Uco Valley), Canada, Chile, Eastern Europe (Bulgaria, Croatia, Moldova, Romania), France (Bordeaux, Southern France), Italy (Friuli-Venezia Giulia, Tuscany), Switzerland (Ticino), United States (California, Long Island, Virginia, Washington State)

IF YOU LIKE THIS, TRY: *Grenache/Garnacha, Malbec, Syrah/Shiraz*

Beyond Bordeaux: France's Famous Blending Grapes

France's Bordeaux is the benchmark region for red wine blends, particularly those based on Merlot and Cabernet Sauvignon. But Bordeaux has five main grapes blended into most of its red wines: Cabernet Franc, Merlot, Cabernet Sauvignon, Malbec, and Petit Verdot. In this tasting, we'll look at what each of those individual grapes brings to those blends, and how they stand out on their own.

Domaine Paul Buisse Chinon (Loire Valley, France)
The Chinon region in France's Loire Valley specializes in reds made primarily from Cabernet Franc grapes. Ruby-red in color, this wine opens with herbal spice and red fruit notes in a forward style. Medium-bodied on the palate, blackberry and red currant flavors dominate. It's that herbal spiciness, however, that is really what this variety is known to bring to blends.

Bonterra Organically Grown Merlot (California)
Dark violet in the glass, plummy on the nose, and medium-bodied and round in the mouth, this wine shows immediately what Merlot can add to a wine blend: namely, body and fruitiness. Juicy cherry and cassis flavors move to hints of vanilla and smoke, courtesy of some oak aging.

Odfjell Armador Organic Cabernet Sauvignon (Maipo Valley, Chile)
Red fruits dominate the nose and flavors (and ruby-red dominates the color), plus there are intriguing notes of licorice, herbs, and mint, and good structure on a full body while retaining good freshness. You can see why this grape is often the backbone of Bordeaux's long-lived red wines.

Domaine Bousquet Tupungato Malbec (Mendoza, Argentina)
A deep violet color lets you know that you're in for a full-bodied drinking experience in this Malbec. Blackberry, tobacco, and plum notes jump from the glass, with violet aromas, moving to a palate full of power and red and black plum flavors. The power, fruitiness, and aromas are all great components to have in putting together a red wine blend.

Ruca Malen 'Terroir Series' Luján de Cuyo Petit Verdot (Mendoza, Argentina)
Baking spices, violets, and dark fruits mark the nose on this inky, purple, full-bodied powerhouse red. Chocolate, cassis, and spiced plum flavors are all over the palate, which is big, tannic, and chewy. A little bit of Petit Verdot can go a long way in rounding out a red blend.

MONASTRELL/MOURVÈDRE

moe/nah/STRELL (more/VEH/drha)

Full-bodied and blood-red Monastrell is Spain's drop-dead serious red grape. Known as Mourvèdre in France, it's found success throughout that country, particularly in the Rhône Valley where it is part of blends from famous red wine regions like Châteauneuf-du-Pape and Côtes du Rhône, and also in Provençal rosés. It's now grown almost anywhere that the climate is warm and dry enough to ripen it properly.

Monastrell works exceedingly well with Grenache and Syrah, so much so that it's part of the well-used acronym GSM (Grenache-Syrah-Mourvèdre), adding structure, mouthfeel, and color to those blended reds. Monastrell is full-bodied, intensely colored, and usually tannic. (In France, it's sometimes called *étrangle-chien*—"the dog strangler"—due to its mouth-drying qualities.) While its palate can be big and rustic, its nose can add interesting complexity, with hints of violets, pepper, and smoked game meats.

Range of possible flavors: Blackberry, blueberry, pepper, violet, smoked meat

Wines that use this grape: Bandol, Châteauneuf-du-Pape, Corbières (Languedoc-Roussillon), Côtes du Rhône

Major production areas: Australia, France (Languedoc-Roussillon, Provence, Rhône Valley, especially Châteauneuf-du-Pape, Côtes du Rhône), Spain (Alicante, Jumilla), United States (California)

IF YOU LIKE THIS, TRY: *Alicante Bouschet, Malbec, Touriga Nacional*

MONTEPULCIANO

maan/tuh/pul/chee/AH/no

Not to be confused with Tuscany's Vino Nobile di Montepulciano wine (which is actually named after a town and made from Sangiovese), the Montepulciano grape is one of the most widely planted in Italy, dominating in the south of that country where the warmer climate allows it to fully ripen. It's marked by a full body, deep ruby color, mouthwatering acidity, and smooth-as-silk tannins.

Montepulciano's plummy red fruit flavors are hard to resist. Combined with a spicy nose and palate freshness, few wines can match it when it comes to pairing with hearty Italian fare. In premium versions from Montepulciano d'Abruzzo, it can be used to create big, concentrated wines with ample tannins, meant to be aged for a few years in bottle (before preferably pairing them with a nice steak).

Range of possible flavors: Red plum, cherry, pizza spices, bramble, tar

Wines that use this grape: Montepulciano d'Abruzzo, Rosso Piceno Superiore

Major production areas: Argentina, Italy (Tuscany, southern Italy, including Abruzzo, Apulia, Emilia-Romagna, Lazio, Marche, Molise, and Umbria), United States

IF YOU LIKE THIS, TRY: *Grenache/Garnacha, Malbec, Merlot*

MUSCAT BLANC

MUHS/kat BLAHN

Muscat (*Moscato* in Italian) is one of the oldest wine grape varieties, dating back to ancient Egypt and Persia. Muscat is actually an umbrella term, containing about 200 varieties, some of which aren't technically related to one another. Usually when talking about Muscat, we're referring to the Muscat Blanc à Petits Grains and Muscat of Alexandria varieties.

Muscat is made in varying styles, but is often pale gold in the glass, with low acidity, light body, and some sweetness in the mouth. Its distinctive aromatic intensity is thanks to a compound called linalool (also found in mint, flowers, and some spices). Few wines can match Muscat for its powerful grapey and floral aromas, which leap out of the glass. Muscat grapes even taste good right off the vine (and have often been used as table grapes).

Muscat Blanc can be found in off-dry spritzy wines (Moscato d'Asti), sparkling versions (Asti Spumante), and many variations of dessert wines, including Muscat de Rivesaltes and Muscat de Beaumes de Venise in France. Muscat of Alexandria has been made into luscious, figgy dessert wines, particularly in Rutherglen (Australia) and South Africa (where it's called "Hanepoot") and (under the name Zibibbo) in the dried-grape *passito* dessert wines of Sicily's Pantelleria island. Other Muscat varieties are made into dessert wines in Greece (Muscat of Samos) and Spain (Moscatel de Setúbal). You get the picture; the long history and success of the Muscat "family" means that they have traveled the world (and then some).

Range of possible flavors: Grape, flowers, rose petals, mandarin, geranium

Wines that use this grape: Asti Spumante, Moscato d'Asti, Vin de Constance (South Africa)

Major production areas: Australia (Rutherglen), Italy (Asti), South Africa, Spain, United States (California)

IF YOU LIKE THIS, TRY: *Pinot Blanc, Pinot Gris/Pinot Grigio, Riesling*

NEBBIOLO

neh/bee/OW/low

Pale garnet in the glass, intense in acidity and mouth-puckering tannins, and big in body, Nebbiolo is considered the most noble of Italian red grape varieties. It is grown primarily in Piedmont, in Northwest Italy, where it is used to produce burly Barolo and slightly more feminine Barbaresco wines. Its name comes from *nebbia* ("fog" in Italian), probably for the fog that sets into the region during harvest. Nebbiolo is old, too; Pliny the Elder referenced what is believed to be Nebbiolo back in the 1st century CE.

Nebbiolo creates some of Piedmont's most long-lived red wines.

The most accessible Nebbiolo wines are usually from Piedmont's Langhe area, with sour cherry flavors, rose petal aromas, and significant but tamed tannins. The big bad daddy is Barolo, a wine that evokes tar, earth, leather, and anise, and in some cases needs several years in the bottle before it softens enough to drink. In any case, Nebbiolo combines power and elegance in a way that few other red grapes can manage.

Range of possible flavors: Sour cherry, leather, earth, roses, anise, tar, leather, coffee

Wines that use this grape: Barbaresco, Barolo, Carema, Gattinara, Ghemme, Roero

Major production areas: Australia, Italy (Piedmont), Mexico, United States

IF YOU LIKE THIS, TRY: *Sagrantino, Sangiovese*

PETITE SIRAH

peh/TEET sih/RAH

Petite Sirah—named after the small size of its berries on the vine—is sometimes called Durif, after François Durif (who discovered a new grape in his nursery in the 1800s, probably an accidental cross-pollination between Peloursin and Syrah). An opaque reddish-purple, Petite Sirah wines can be some of the burliest reds in the wine business. Theoretically, they are also some of the healthiest, being naturally high in antioxidants (as well as in acids and tannins).

Petite Sirah is the kind of wine that stains your teeth and coats your gums, presenting a powerful presence in the mouth with its structure and body. It's a great match for grilled meats, such as flank steak, as its tannins help soften the texture of proteins.

Range of possible flavors: Plum, blueberry, black tea, chocolate, black pepper

Wines that use this grape: Blended into many Cabernet Sauvignon wines; also bottled varietally in Argentina, Brazil, California, Chile, France, Israel, and Mexico

Major production areas: Australia, United States (California)

IF YOU LIKE THIS, TRY: *Sagrantino, Tannat*

PINOT GRIS/PINOT GRIGIO

PEE/noh GREE (PEE/noh GREE/jo)

Ubiquitous almost to the point of parody, Pinot Gris (named after the grayish-pink tint in its grape skins) has seen such popularity that it is now grown in just about every winemaking country around the globe. While its overripe examples from hot climates tend to deserve their poor reputation, Pinot Gris/Grigio from cooler areas (such as Trentino-Alto Adige in northern Italy, Alsace in France, and several areas of New Zealand) offer lighter- to medium-bodied white wines—across the spectrum from dry to sweet—that can be pure delight.

Pinot Gris, named for the pinkish-gray hue of its ripened grapes.

Usually golden to copper in color, good Pinot Gris evokes lemons, limes, and green apples, as well as nectarine and melon, and sometimes offers floral aromas. Sweeter versions can add lemon-drop and tropical fruit flavors, evolving to notes of honey and toasted nut after aging. Pinot Gris lovers should never shoulder a sense of shame; after all, this is a grape that is capable of producing some of the most storied Grand Cru wines of Alsace (on the richer side), as well as refreshing, vibrant, and delectable whites (as in northern Italy).

Range of possible flavors: Citrus, apple, melon, nectarine, white flowers

Wines that use this grape: Varietal dry and sweet wines from Alsace, California, Northeastern Italy, and New Zealand

Major production areas: Austria, France (Alsace), Germany, Italy (especially Trentino-Alto Adige), New Zealand, also . . . pretty much every other winemaking country!

IF YOU LIKE THIS, TRY: *Albariño, Chenin Blanc, Grenache Blanc*

Shades of Gray: Pinot Gris/Grigio

There's an old joke in the wine business that "Pinot Grigio" is Italian for "I have no flavor" (it actually is named after the color of the gray-tinged grapes in its bunches). Pinot Grigio (aka Pinot Gris or Grauburgunder) has a bad rep, but it's mostly unwarranted. Here are a few wines that prove that this grape is capable of deliciousness in the right hands.

Peter Zemmer Pinot Grigio (Alto Adige, Italy)

Northern Italy is the spiritual home of Pinot Grigio. This PG is a great example, too; a greenish straw color, with aromas of pear and white flowers, with medium body and a lovely interplay of minerality and ripe melon flavors.

Hugel 'Classic' Pinot Gris (Alsace, France)

France's Alsace is a charming place, and this is a charming wine. Straw-yellow in hue, it opens with ginger and star fruit notes, followed by melon flavors, zesty lemon peel acidity, and balanced elegance.

Mt. Beautiful Pinot Gris (North Canterbury, New Zealand)

New Zealand can produce Pinot Gris that's fuller-bodied but retains excellent freshness. Mt. Beautiful's lemon-yellow version lives up to its name, with gorgeous lavendar aromas, hints of tropical fruits, and zesty red apple flavors on a rich palate.

Willamette Valley Vineyards Pinot Gris (Willamette Valley, Oregon)

While Oregon is best known for Pinot Noir, its Pinot Gris wines can also be stellar. This complex white wine is a deep yellow, opens with green apple, nut, and honeysuckle aromas, and finishes with a sense of creamy weight, balanced by citrus flavors.

J Vineyards & Winery Pinot Gris (California)

This wine is a perennial wonder, blending grapes from across California to consistently produce a ripe, rich, interesting Pinot Gris. Greenish-yellow in color, there are tropical fruit and white flower notes jumping out of the glass. Melon, citrus, and ripe pear flavors abound, and the wine feels substantial in the mouth, but not too big, making it a great match for shellfish.

PINOT NOIR

pee/no N'WAR

Pinot Noir makes arguably the most elegant wines in the world. It certainly makes the most expensive, and not just because it's a primary component of Champagne; Pinot Noir is used to create the most exclusive red wines of Burgundy, made in tiny quantities and fetching thousands of dollars per bottle.

Pinot Noir's name comes from the French for black pine, describing its tightly bunched grape clusters. Those clusters, and their thinner skins, make Pinot susceptible to several vine maladies, so the grape is difficult to grow and often becomes a labor of love for its high-end producers. Its acidity is the backbone of the world's best sparkling wines, particularly those from Champagne, where it adds structure, color, and red berry nuances.

Pinot Noir is usually transparent ruby-red in the glass, with medium body, lighter tannins, and good acidity. Elegance and poise are the big draws here, and few Pinot wines are bombastic (though some can be bigger and intense, such as those from Sonoma's Russian River Valley). Red fruits abound, as do aromas of tea, hibiscus, and earth. Pinot Noir's earthiness tends to increase as it ages, taking on truffle and "forest floor" qualities while retaining a tart, red plum core.

Due to its finicky nature, good entry-level Pinots aren't that easy to find, but you can start with examples from Oregon, Sonoma County, and New Zealand (which still offer good value) before deciding to take out a second mortgage on more famous red Burgundies.

Range of possible flavors: Cherry, red berries, truffle, earth, tea, flowers, "forest floor"

Wines that use this grape: Red Burgundy (Puligny-Montrachet, Pommard, Volnay, Bourgogne Rouge, Côte Chalonnaise, and others), Champagne (Blanc de Noirs, rosé), Franciacorta

Major production areas: Australia (Adelaide Hills, Great Southern, Mornington Peninsula, Tasmania, Yarra Valley), France (Burgundy, Champagne), Italy (Franciacorta), New Zealand (Central Otago, Marlborough, Martinborough), South Africa (Elgin, Walker Bay), United States (California, including Alexander Valley, Carneros, Russian River Valley, Sonoma County; Oregon, especially Willamette Valley)

IF YOU LIKE THIS, TRY: *Barbera, Gamay*

PINOTAGE

PEE/no/tajh

Perhaps no red wine grape is as divisive as Pinotage. Fuller-bodied and often tannic, with a dark red plum color in the glass, Pinotage requires care in the vineyard, as it can otherwise produce wines that are tough, burly, and reminiscent of acetone.

It was created as a cross in South Africa in 1925 by Professor Abraham Izak Perold, who was looking to combine the heartiness of Cinsault (aka Hermitage) with the elegance of Pinot Noir. Pinotage was thus born and quickly became the second-most-planted grape in South Africa (despite bearing hardly any resemblance to its forebears). When made well, Pinotage can be a real thinking person's sipper, combining deep red color, a hearty palate, and a fascinating assemblage of spice, smoke, and game notes.

Range of possible flavors: Blackberry, mulberry, smoke, bramble, soil, leather, hoisin, smoked meat

Wines that use this grape: Varietal and red blends from South Africa

Major production areas: Brazil, South Africa, United States

IF YOU LIKE THIS, TRY: *Carménère, Malbec*

RIESLING

REEZ/ling

Native to Germany's Rhine region, Riesling creates wines that are usually light-bodied and highly aromatic, and possess levels of acidity that feel almost electric. It's made into just about every style, from sparkling Sekt in Germany to off-dry, dry, sweet, and succulent dessert wines (including Icewine, an amazing treat from cold climates where grapes freeze on the vine, concentrating their sugars). Riesling's energetic palate often demands that some residual sugar is left in order to make the palate balanced (rather than feeling like someone spiked your wine with battery acid). If ever there was a wine that could wake up your senses, Riesling is it.

Riesling: one of the most diverse and aromatic of all white wine grapes

Riesling grapes need a long, cool ripening season to fully mature. This makes it particularly well suited to Germany, Austria, and New York's Finger Lakes. Aromas and flavors vary, but you can almost always find citrus, tree fruit, and stone fruit flavors with flower and mineral notes. Its colors range from straw (in youth) to amber yellow (with age). Speaking of aging—despite its lower alcohol and body, Riesling often contains enough structure in its acidity and sugar to spend time in the bottle (in some cases, decades).

Range of possible flavors: Apple, citrus, tree fruits, stone fruits, flowers, ginger, jasmine, minerals, smoke, honey, gasoline

Wines that use this grape: Austrian and German Sekt sparkling wines, varietal wines from Alsace, Australia, Austria, Germany, and the United States

Major production areas: Australia (Clare Valley, Eden Valley), Austria, Canada, France (Alsace), Germany (Mosel, Nahe, Pfalz, Rheingau), United States (California, Michigan, New York State Finger Lakes, Washington State)

IF YOU LIKE THIS, TRY: *Gewürztraminer, Muscat Blanc, Pinot Blanc, Sauvignon Blanc*

Riesling: Dry to Sweet

Riesling is often thought of only as a dessert wine, but its different global incarnations prove that there's much more to this noble grape. Let's explore Riesling's various styles, from bone dry to lip-smacking sweet.

Jim Barry Lodge Hill Riesling (Clare Valley, Australia)

Clare Valley is known for producing Rieslings that have low residual sugars. This lively, bracing, light-bodied example is a pale straw color, with vibrant lime and ginger aromas and flavors of pear and citrus. It's lean and focused in the mouth and will get you rethinking Riesling's sweeter reputation.

Dr. Konstantin Frank Semi-Dry Riesling (Finger Lakes, New York)

This is now one of America's iconic wines: Dr. Konstantin Frank helped put the Finger Lakes region on the world wine map, especially for growing premium versions of this grape. Pale gold and light-bodied, this Riesling's residual sugar is balanced by its acidity, giving a lively mouthfeel that also has roundness. It's full of white flower and citrus aromas, and ample lime and apple flavors with a hint of lemon-drop candy.

Carl Graff Graacher Himmelreich Riesling Spätlese (Mosel, Germany)

From Germany's most famous Riesling area comes this gold-yellow bargain of a white, with mandarin orange, lemon zest, and apricot aromas. The palate is light and has verve due to its acidity, but is also soft on the edges thanks to all of the sugar. (Germany's Spätlese category indicates fully ripened grapes and is often medium-sweet in style.) Ripe melon, pear, and apple flavors round things out in the mouth.

Hogue Late Harvest Riesling (Columbia Valley, Washington State)

Washington State has little problem bringing wine grapes to full ripeness, which allows the creation of luscious late harvest dessert expressions of Riesling, like this one from Hogue. This wine could be dessert on its own or paired with fruit-based desserts. It has golden hues, a medium-bodied palate, and lots of sweetness. Flavors of tangerine candy and apricots are topped by mineral, lemon, lime, and orange aromas that even smell ripe and juicy. Through it all, you will still get Riesling's signature refreshing acidity.

SANGIOVESE

san/joh/VAY/zeh

With its moderate to high tannins, high acidity, medium body, red fruits, and light ruby color, Sangiovese is the foodie's red wine. Its name means "blood of Jove," a reference to Jupiter, and its use might even predate Roman times to the reign of the Etruscans. In other words, Sangiovese has some serious history behind it.

Your first encounter with Sangiovese will likely be in the wines of Chianti, central Tuscany's most popular red. Many of these are plummy, vivacious, earthy, and easy to drink, pairing great with pizza and pasta dishes (similar styles can be found in the reds of Emilia-Romagna). But Sangiovese has much more to offer for the curious, and at the highest levels its wines can compete with the best reds in all of Italy.

Being an older variety, Sangiovese has many clonal variations. Its most famous offshoot is Brunello, the grape behind the tannic, complex wines of Brunello di Montalcino. Sangiovese is also used to make the heady, powerful Vino Nobile di Montepulciano and its bigger, spicier side can be found in the recently added Chianti Classico Gran Selezione designation, meant for exceptional wines with aging potential.

Range of possible flavors: Red plum, sour cherry, strawberry, thyme, spices, dried orange peel, tobacco, leather, earth

Wines that use this grape: Brunello di Montalcino, Chianti (including Chianti Classico, Chianti Classico Riserva, Chianti Classico Gran Selezione), Patrimonio, Sangiovese di Romagna, Vino Nobile di Montepulciano, and varietal wines worldwide

Major production areas: Corsica, Israel, Italy (Chianti, Emilia-Romagna, Lazio, Montepulciano, Tuscany), United States (California, Oregon, Washington State)

IF YOU LIKE THIS, TRY: *Nebbiolo, Syrah/Shiraz*

SAUVIGNON BLANC

SOH/vihn/yohn BLAHN

One of the most aromatic of all wine grapes, Sauvignon Blanc ("wild white" in French) is almost always golden-colored, high in acidity, and low to medium in body. However, this is a grape that takes on different nuances depending on where it is grown.

Sauvignon Blanc wines are noted for high acidity and exuberant flavors.

Cooler-climate Sauvignon Blanc (notably from South Africa and Chile) tends toward citrus flavors and vegetal, herbal notes. Warmer climes give richer wines, with tropical fruit and melon flavors, sometimes with more body (as in Napa Valley) or even seeing wood aging (as in Mondavi's famous Fumé Blanc). In the middle, we have Sauvignon's sweet spot—literally, in the case of the incredible, long-lived dessert wines of Sauternes and Barsac in France.

Dry versions from Bordeaux tend to be expensive, as they have the ability to age in the bottle and are justifiably famous. France's Loire offers two very unique takes on the grape, in the dainty and lively Sancerre Blanc, and in the gunflint spiciness of Pouilly-Fumé. Most people, however, will (and should) start their Sauvignon journey with wines from New Zealand; these are highly aromatic, with intense, pure passion fruit and grass aromas and an easily accessible, vibrant palate.

Range of possible flavors: Tropical fruits, apple, nectarine, peach, citrus, white flowers, grass, straw, herbs, exotic fruits, vegetables, gunflint

Wines that use this grape: Barsac (for sweet wines), Bordeaux Blanc, Entre-Deux-Mers, Pouilly-Fumé, Sancerre Blanc, Sauternes (for sweet wines), Sauvignon de Touraine

Major production areas: Chile, Italy (Friuli-Venezia Giulia), France (Bordeaux, Loire Valley), New Zealand, South Africa, United States (California)

IF YOU LIKE THIS, TRY: *Albariño, Riesling, Torrontés*

SÉMILLON

say/mee/YAWN

Sémillon is most known for its role in France's Bordeaux region. Though that area is dominated by red wine production, Sémillon is one of the grapes permitted in Bordeaux Blanc, where it goes into some of the most famous and long-lived white wines in the world. It's also a key component in Sauternes, perhaps the most coveted dessert wine ever, in which grapes affected by "noble rot" (see page 24) are hand-picked to create an unforgettable—and expensive—drinking experience.

As a dry white wine, Sémillon tends to be golden in the glass, with low acidity and a medium to large body. This has led many a wine writer to describe its viscous texture as "oily." From cooler regions, Sémillon wines show more apple and citrus flavors and straw and lanolin notes; warmer areas produce wines that have more tropical fruit flavors. If ever there was a "grounding" white wine, Sémillon is it.

Range of possible flavors: Apple, citrus, pear, tropical fruits, lanolin, straw, ginger, white flowers

Wines that use this grape: Bordeaux Blanc, Sauternes

Major production areas: Australia (Hunter Valley), France (Bordeaux), South Africa

IF YOU LIKE THIS, TRY: *Albariño, Chenin Blanc, Pinot Gris/Pinot Grigio, Viognier*

SYRAH/SHIRAZ

see/RAH (shuh/RAAZ)

Despite its Persian-sounding name, Syrah (often called Shiraz in Australia) is probably of French origin, and France is its leading producer (with planting amounts exploding there since the 1960s). It dominates the red wines of the sunny, windy Rhône Valley, and is often blended with Grenache and Mourvèdre in both reds and rosés. In the Rhône it can even be co-fermented with white grapes, bringing aromatic lift to the finished red wine.

Syrah is usually plummy and juicy, with full body, medium tannin, and medium to low acidity, and bursting with blackberry and blueberry flavors. One of its calling cards is a spicy peppercorn note, which prevails (along with aromas of dried herbs) when it's grown in cooler areas.

As Shiraz, Syrah has absolutely overrun Australia; it is the country's most planted variety, making Australia the second-largest producer of Syrah after France. Their versions tend toward jammier fruit flavors, with distinctive mint and eucalyptus notes. While many simple, forgettable Shiraz wines have flooded the market, Australia is still home to some of the greatest red wines in all of the Southern Hemisphere, sourced from Syrah vines that can be more than a century old.

Range of possible flavors: Blueberry, blackberry, bramble, peppercorns, dried herbs, smoked meat, chocolate, cigar, eucalyptus

Wines that use this grape: Cornas, Côtes-du-Rhône, Côte-Rôtie, Crozes-Hermitage, Hermitage, Saint-Joseph, Southern Rhône reds (including Châteauneuf-du-Pape)

Major production areas: Argentina, Australia (especially Barossa Valley, McLaren Vale), Chile, France (Languedoc-Roussillon, Rhône Valley), Italy (Apulia, Lazio, Tuscany), New Zealand, South Africa, United States (California, Washington State)

IF YOU LIKE THIS, TRY: *Grenache, Merlot, Petite Sirah*

TEMPRANILLO

tehm/prah/NEE/yoh

It's a testament to the success of Tempranillo that it has more synonyms than almost any other grape variety. The Rioja region's king of red grapes is known as Cencibel, Tinto del País, Tinta de Toro, Piñuela, Tinta de Nava, Ull de Llebre, and Chinchillana. And all of those are just from other regions within Spain. In nearby Portugal, Tempranillo is known as Aragonês or Tinta Roriz and goes into some of the country's best Port wines.

Tempranillo is Spain's most-planted wine grape variety.

While an intrepid world traveler, Tempranillo shines brightest at home (most likely originating in La Rioja). Spanish speakers might have already guessed that Tempranillo's name was probably adapted from *temprano* ("early"), as it both buds and ripens before most red varieties.

In the glass, Tempranillo gives medium alcohol and body, medium acidity, and ample but easy-to-drink tannins, with flavors ranging from wild strawberries (at entry level) to darker plums and black cherries (in premium versions). This grape exudes class right out of the gate, with aromas of spices, leather, and a signature hint of tobacco. In Rioja, Tempranillo often gains toast, coconut, cigar, and cedar aromas and a softer mouthfeel from oak aging.

Tempranillo's most exciting feature is how long-lived the best wines made from it can be, especially from great vintages sourced from older vines.

Range of possible flavors: Red and black cherries, strawberry, plum, spices, leather, tobacco

Wines that use this grape: Alentejo reds, Douro reds, Port, Rioja

Major production areas: Argentina, Mexico, Portugal (Alentejo, Douro, Porto), Spain (Ribera del Duero, Rioja), United States (Arizona, California, Oregon, Texas, Washington State)

IF YOU LIKE THIS, TRY: *Grenache/Garnacha, Monastrell/Mourvèdre, Sangiovese*

The Tiers of Tempranillo in Rioja

Tempranillo from Rioja, Spain, comes in a few very distinct styles, making it one of the most user-friendly wines with which to experiment and explore. Here's a tasting of the major Rioja levels, all featuring Tempranillo as their backbone.

El Coto Rioja Rosé

Tempranillo has a softer side, as you'll find in this rosé made from grapes in Rioja Alavesa. Watermelon-red in the glass, rose petal, strawberry, and citrus peel aromas mingle with a vibrant, lively palate to make this a great budget pick for pink.

CVNE Cune Crianza Rioja

This venerable producer has great buys across the board, but their zesty, pure, Crianza-style red is a standout. Rioja's Crianza wines are aged one year in oak, giving this garnet-colored wine tinges of wood spices that add class to its fresh, red berry fruit flavors and medium body. You'll want tapas with this one—it's one of Rioja's culinary specialties and so tends to be a great pairing with the region's wines.

Muga Rioja Reserva

Muga has been crafting Rioja since the 1930s and their expertise is well on display in this Tempranillo blend. A unique middle-ground category between younger Crianza and more developed, oak-aged Gran Reserva, Rioja Reserva wines see slightly extended oak aging. In this case, the oak gives bricked edges to this ruby-red wine, as well as depth to its mouthfeel, and vanilla notes to its tobacco-laden nose. You'll find raspberry and dark cherry flavors to spare and a mouthfeel that is balanced and delicious.

Beronia Gran Reserva Rioja

Rioja's Gran Reserva category mandates a minimum of two years of oak aging and three years of bottle aging. The result? You get a premium red wine that takes the guesswork out of when it's ready to drink, since the bodega or cellar has done most of the aging for you! Gran Reserva reds can be a wonderful treat, such as this one by Beronia. Almost orange-tinged in the glass, cedar, spice, coconut, vanilla, and cigar aromas waft up. In the mouth, this is all dark fruit grandeur, with power and a sense of focus from its fine acidity. For a further treat, open it with hearty fare, like a roast.

VIOGNIER

vee/oh/NYAY

Usually full-bodied, lush, and presenting lovely shades of gold, Viognier is the grape to which Chardonnay lovers turn when they want something different. Like Chardonnay, Viognier can be found in lighter, more vibrant forms (as from Virginia), but is more often encountered in oaked versions that show ripe tropical fruit flavors (and can even be found in luscious, almost syrupy late-harvest dessert wines). It has abundant floral aromas (think honeysuckle and white roses), as well as a pleasant astringency that, when handled correctly in the winemaking process, can add a sense of structure and "bite" to its broad mouthfeel.

While Viognier might have originated in Dalmatia (in present-day Croatia), and is now found all over the winemaking world, it reaches its heights in France's Rhône Valley, particularly in the age-worthy wines of Condrieu (where it is the only white grape permitted to be used).

Range of possible flavors: Peach, tangerine, tropical fruits, white flowers, rose petals

Wines that use this grape: Condrieu (France), many white blends from Australia, late-harvest dessert wines

Major production areas: Australia, France (Rhône Valley), Israel, South Africa, United States (California)

IF YOU LIKE THIS, TRY: *Chardonnay, Grenache Blanc*

ZINFANDEL

ZIN/fuhn/del

Zinfandel is often cited as the quintessential "American" red grape (thriving in the United States both before and after Prohibition), but its DNA profile shows it's an adopted son. Zinfandel is actually identical to Crljenak Kaštelanski and Tribidrag (from Croatia) and Primitivo (from southern Italy). The proliferation of Zin plantings in California in recent decades can be traced back to Sutter Home Winery's Bob Trinchero, who in 1972 created a sweet/blush rendition called White Zinfandel. This reddish-pink rosé—light in body, sweet to the taste, and reminiscent of watermelon flavors—still accounts for over 80 percent of Zinfandel production in the United States.

Red Zinfandel, however, is a dry wine, deep ruby in color, heavy in body, and bursting with dark fruit flavors (from black cherry to raisin). Zinfandel grape bunches tend to ripen unevenly, meaning that underripe and overripe grapes can be harvested along with fully ripened grapes, sometimes in the same bunch. This phenomenon creates jammy fruit flavors to the resulting wine, as well as aromas that range from peppery to raisiny. That combination of power, easy drinkability, and spicy complexity has made Zinfandel a favorite red wine among US consumers.

Range of possible flavors: Black raspberry, black currant, black cherry, blueberry jam, raisin, fig, plums, pepper, cardamom, licorice

Wines that use this grape: Varietal wines and field blends throughout California, also White Zinfandel

Major production areas: Italy (Apulia, where it's called Primitivo), United States (California, including Amador, Lodi, Napa Valley, Paso Robles, San Luis Obispo, Santa Cruz Mountains, Sonoma County)

IF YOU LIKE THIS, TRY: *Negroamaro*

ELEVEN LESSER-KNOWN GRAPE VARIETIES TO EXPLORE

If you're looking to go beyond the usual wine grape suspects, here are a few of my favorite off-the-beaten-path grape varieties, all making exciting wines.

WHITE

Assyrtiko: Makes fresh, heady white wines from the gorgeous Greek island of Santorini

Carricante: This zesty, complex variety makes some of the best white wines in all of Sicily

Furmint: Hungary's versatile grape, long used in their historically famous Tokaji Aszú dessert wines, is now being made into stunning dry whites as well

Garganega: The main ingredient in Soave, crafting perhaps the perfect white wine for summer sipping

Marsanne: The Northern Rhône's answer to Chardonnay

Vermentino: Citric and nutty, this is one of Italy's hidden-gem white wine grapes

RED

Agiorgitiko: This variety, indigenous to the Peloponnese in Greece, makes spicy, lush reds

Nero d'Avola: This red is to Sicily what Cabernet Sauvignon is to Napa Valley

Petit Verdot: Used to beef up many red wine blends, PV combines delicate floral notes with burly palate texture

Sagrantino: Italy's spicy, dark match for gourmet burgers

Tannat: This burly red grape first came to prominence in the Basque-influenced areas of France, particularly in Madiran. It's now grown worldwide, and has taken especially well to the climate of Uruguay. It's extremely high in tannins (and, therefore, in antioxidants), and makes an ideal wine for those who love their reds big and powerful.

Garganega grapes are used to make Soave, a vibrant white wine produced in Italy's historic Veneto region.

CHAPTER 3

WINEMAKING AND FLAVOR

Winemakers will tell you that you can't make great wine from bad grapes, but you can definitely make bad wine from great grapes. After grapes, the winemaking process has the next-largest impact on the flavors that you will encounter in the glass—and winemakers only get one chance per year (during harvest) to get it right.

Here's an introduction to how different styles of wine are made in the cellar. As we walk through a wine's journey from grape to glass, we'll explore why each of the winemaking steps are so important to determining how a wine tastes, feels, smells, and ages.

The Winemaking Process

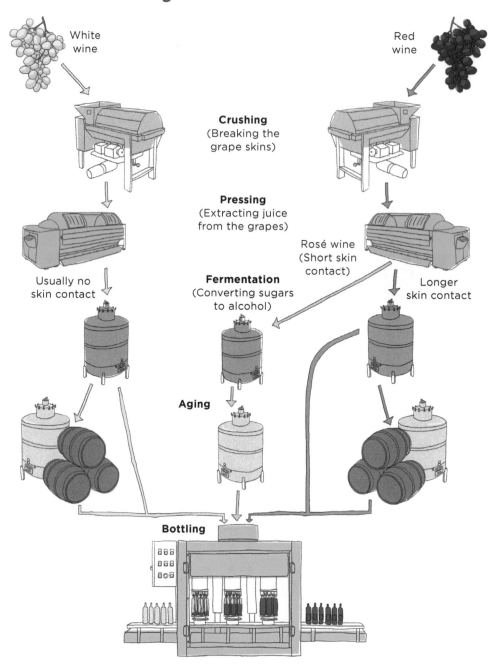

White wine

Red wine

Crushing
(Breaking the grape skins)

Pressing
(Extracting juice from the grapes)

Rosé wine
(Short skin contact)

Usually no skin contact

Fermentation
(Converting sugars to alcohol)

Longer skin contact

Aging

Bottling

Crushing, Soaking, and Pressing

Vinification (the portion of winemaking that takes place in the cellar) happens as soon as harvested grapes arrive at the winery (usually transported in shallow containers, so that no grapes are crushed prematurely). Ideally, the grapes have been protected from oxidation (overexposure to air, which can cause color and odor issues, especially in white grapes) en route to the winery.

Once they arrive and before fermentation begins, grapes are sorted (sometimes manually, often via automated process) to remove subpar fruit (and the occasional vineyard critter or two). From there, the winemaking steps vary depending on the type of wine being made—and that's our next stop in the flavor journey.

WHITE WINES

For white wines, the most important first step is that the grapes arrive with their skins intact, so that ambient yeasts don't start fermenting the grape sugars early. Next, the winemaker may decide to crush and destem the berries, rather than press the berries whole (more on that in a minute). This helps the

The grapes are usually destemmed before pressing, as the stems can impart bitterness.

extraction of flavor from the grape must, which is the grape juice including the grape skins, seeds, and stems, that will result after pressing. Crushing breaks the berries without breaking the seeds inside (they can impart unwanted bitter flavors), while destemming is used to separate the berries from the stems (which can add bitterness to the wine, too).

White wines typically will be kept from making contact with the grape skins (this contact is always done for red wines). In some cases, there might be flavor elements from the skins that the winemaker wants to impart into a white or rosé wine, in which case the grapes will be "cold soaked" before pressing. This is like getting a head start on extracting color and flavor from the grapes and is done for a few days at cold temperatures (usually under 50 degrees Fahrenheit), to prevent any yeasts from fermenting the grape sugars into alcohol.

Grape pressing requires careful timing and a gentle touch to ensure high-quality wine.

The next step is pressing—extracting the juice from the grapes. Generally, temperatures need to be between 55 and 75 degrees Fahrenheit during this step. Pressing can be done via several methods, but in every case, the focus is to make the process as gentle as possible. While pressing doesn't take a very long time (and needs to be quick, to avoid oxidizing the juice), it has a direct and disproportionately large impact on the quality of the eventual wine.

White and rosé wines often go through a settling process, to help remove solid material from the must. This can be done by holding the juice in tanks at very cold (almost freezing) temperatures, during which unwanted sediment falls to the bottom of the tank and is removed.

ROSÉ WINES

Rosés follow the same pre-fermentation process as white wines, with two exceptions. First, rosés are usually made from red wine grapes that have been picked early to retain natural acidity. Second, rosés will see a brief period of skin contact, to get just a bit of color and flavor from the compounds found in the grape skins. Grapes meant for rosé production might also undergo the cold-soaking step described on the preceding page.

Alternatively, the *saignée* ("bleeding") method can be used to produce rosé. In this method, some of the juice is "bled" from red wine must after it has macerated (had contact with the skins of the grapes) for a short period of time. That juice is then vinified much like a white wine.

What about blending finished white and red wine into a rosé? That's actually illegal by most winemaking regulations (the end result usually isn't all that great), except in Champagne, where reds and whites can be blended before undergoing secondary fermentation.

Think Pink: The Surprising Diversity of Rosé

If you think that pink wines are all watered-down, sweet versions of Zinfandel, then you're missing out on some of the best wine experiences out there. Rosé is made from nearly every red grape, and in this tasting you'll get a feel for just how diverse the modern rosé market is.

Domaine de Cala Coteaux Varois en Provence (Provence, France)

Every wine lover's rosé journey should start with the south of France, the benchmark region for dry rosé. Domaine de Cala's Provençal rosé, blended from Grenache, Syrah, and other varieties, is a perfect introduction to the modern rosé style. It's pale pink, fresh in the mouth, herbal and floral on the nose, and entices with strawberry and lemon zest flavors.

SeaGlass Rosé of Pinot Noir (Central Coast, California)

It makes sense that Pinot Noir, which goes into so many amazing sparkling rosés, should make excellent dry rosé, too. SeaGlass has this dark pink gem, made from Pinot grown in Monterey. Its elegant nose reminds you of dried rose petals, while its zesty mouthfeel offers flavors of just-ripe cherries.

Biohof Pratsch Rosé (Niederösterreich, Austria)

Several varieties of organically grown grapes are used to make this Austrian rosé. It's light red in the glass and smells of peaches and pears. Its flavors mimic its aromas, ending with a wonderful sense of acidic refreshment.

Chateau D'Aqueria Tavel Rosé (Rhône Valley, France)

Tavel is famous for making the red wine lover's rosé. A bright reddish pink color hints at the fuller body that this Grenache, Clairette, Cinsault, and Mourvèdre blend brings, and one sniff of its dark raspberry nose will be enough to get the attention of people who don't usually consider drinking rosé. Watermelon flavors round things out on a long, powerful finish.

Crios de Susana Balbo Rosé of Malbec (Mendoza, Argentina)

The burly Malbec might not seem like an obvious choice for rosé, but in the right hands its brute force can be forged into surprising results. Take this almost blood-red rosé from Susana Balbo's Crios label: it's spicy on the nose, with hints of wild strawberries and bramble. The palate, while fuller for a rosé, is still zesty and flavorful, with dark berries galore.

RED WINES

The main step in red wine vinification is maceration. Without it, almost all red wine grapes would produce a white wine (because with few exceptions, red grapes have clear pulp). Maceration imbues the grape juice with the color, flavor, and structural compounds (i.e., tannins) found in the grape skins.

Maceration continues into the fermentation process (see page 71), and the longer the maceration time, the more flavor, tannins, and color are extracted from the skins and imparted into the juice. For entry-level, fruity wine styles, this process might only last a few days; for bold red wines meant for long-haul bottle aging, maceration might continue for weeks.

When maceration is finished, the juice (now imbued with the desired amount of flavor compounds from the skins) needs to be separated from the must. Typically, this happens by pressing the skins and transferring the juice to a steel tank to complete fermentation (when yeasts will convert the sugars in the juice into alcohol). Sometimes, a small percentage of juice from maceration is run off (called "free run" juice) before pressing. Free run juice is high in quality and may be vinified separately for premium wine or blended back into the "press wine" later.

Tannins

Ever had a cup of tea that's been steeped too long, coating your tongue and mouth with a drying, bitter sensation? That's thanks to tannins, astringent polyphenolic compounds that are found in several plants, including wine grape skins (and grape seeds and stems, and also in the wood barrels in which wine is sometimes aged).

Tannins add structural texture to wine. They also bind with proteins, which is why tannin feels so astringent in your mouth (they literally make your saliva less lubricated) and why tannic red wines taste so good when paired with protein-rich foods, like steak.

Tannin is also a natural antioxidant, so it helps preserve wine for bottle aging (and may have some health benefits for us wine drinkers, too). The thicker the grape skins, and the longer the maceration, the more tannins a red wine will have. Some grape varieties are naturally low in tannins, like Pinot Noir, Gamay, Grenache, and Barbera. Others are tannic monsters, including Nebbiolo, Petite Sirah, and the aptly named Tannat. Many are somewhere in between, like Merlot and Cabernet Sauvignon.

Tannins: A Wine Structure Primer

Pucker up, buttercup! In this tasting, you're going to get familiar with the feeling of tannins, the compounds originating in grape skins that give a wine structure, the ability to age, and oodles of mouth-coating astringency.

Josh Cellars Pinot Noir (Central Coast, California)

Wait, what's this higher acid, low tannin grape doing here? To calibrate your palate, that's what (and provide a palate refresher at the end of the tasting, if you need it—you'll thank me later). While enjoying the sweet oak notes and red berry aroma and flavors (and a lighter red color to match its medium body), pay attention to this red's lack of tannins, which helps emphasize the wine's fruitiness. You might get a hint of structure amid the vibrancy in the palate, but just a hint.

Taylors Wakefield Estate Shiraz (Clare Valley, Australia)

Darker red in the glass, with peppery and meaty aromas, and blueberry and chocolate flavors, this Shiraz will feel round with ample body at first. But leave it in your mouth a bit and you'll start to feel a leather-like "grip." That's thanks to a slightly higher tannin content in the grapes, which was imparted to the wine.

Pedroncelli Petite Sirah (Sonoma County, California)

The dark purple color will start to give it away; with this red you're about to get a lot more tannin action. There's big body here, and tons of blueberry and plum flavors with vanilla and smoke notes. There's also a lot more structure; if you can, let it sit in your mouth for a minute and feel how those tannin molecules start to "dry out" your gums. That structure makes this red a bargain, as it will age well in the bottle, which is a direct result of Petite Sirah's small berry size. Smaller berries mean a higher skin-to-juice ratio for the grapes, and the ability to impart more tannins into the wine.

Garzón Tannat Reserva (Garzón, Uruguay)

Tannat isn't native to Uruguay, but it's found its spiritual home in the terroir of that small South American nation. Tannat is named after tannin, so you can probably guess where this one is going; it has some of the highest tannin amounts of any grape variety. Deeply purple, with tobacco spice on the nose and black fruit flavors in the mouth, everything is amped up here: both the acidity and the tannin. While Garzón manages to evoke elegance from this burly grape, there's no escaping the viselike grip with which the Tannat grape will ensnare your palate!

SPARKLING AND DESSERT WINES

Sparkling and dessert wines are treated the same way as white, rosé, or red wines (depending on the grapes, of course) during this stage of vinification. Their special flavor magic comes later, during fermentation (more on that below).

For now, here's what you need to remember:

- Sparkling wines are usually made with grapes that are high in acidity and lower in potential alcohol. These are made first into a still "base" wine that will later undergo a second fermentation process that will add the bubbles.

- Dessert wines are either made with overripe grapes that are higher in sugars, or the winemaker deliberately interferes with their fermentation to retain or add sugars (which is how fortified wines like Port, Madeira, and Sherry are made).

Fermentation

The main stage in the vinification show is fermentation, during which yeasts convert the sugars in the grape juice into alcohol (and release carbon dioxide and heat). The more sugars—and the riper the grapes—the more potential alcohol the final wine will have. Fermentation also produces aldehydes, acids, glycerol, and esters, all of which impact flavor, texture, and aroma. These are the sources of what are commonly referred to as *secondary* aromas in wine.

Sometimes, winemakers use ambient or wild yeasts (yeasts that occur naturally in the vineyard and the winery) and let the process happen spontaneously. That can create wines with more character but makes the fermentation process less predictable. More commonly, an inoculation of specific yeast strains is used (some meant to enhance particular flavors). Yeasts are finicky about temperature, so that's controlled during fermentation to ensure it's warm enough (about 54 degrees Fahrenheit) for them to multiply and do their thing.

RED WINES

Red wine fermentation begins during maceration and is usually completed after pressing the juice into tanks or barrels. The vessel used depends on the style of wine that the winemaker hopes to achieve, but steel tanks are the most common.

Modern winemaking employs temperature-controlled tanks for fermentation.

Once fermentation begins, things heat up, CO_2 is released (which is why it's important never to fill a winemaking vessel to the brim), and the process continues until the yeasts can't find any more sugars to eat (and die).

Many red wines (and some white wines) then undergo what is known as malolactic fermentation (or ML for short). During ML, lactic bacteria take the malic acid in the wine (which tastes like green apples), convert it into lactic acid (which has a round, creamy texture, like milk), and release more carbon dioxide. Warm (68 degrees Fahrenheit) temperatures are necessary for ML to take place, and it's a crucial step in creating the silky body that is sought after in many premium wines.

Maceration

There are several methods for macerating red wine. If a winemaker wants to extract flavors and colors from the grape skins while minimizing the amount of tannins added to a wine, a "cold soak" (or "cold maceration") can be used before fermentation, just like what's done for some white and rosé wines.

During fermentation, a cap of grape skins forms and needs to be broken and remixed with the juice. This cap can be punched down manually with stirrers

Maceration is a key step for the color, flavor, and structure of red wines.

(or even human feet), or automatically using hydraulics or rotary blades. In some cases, wine from the bottom of the tank is pumped over the cap in a process called *remontage*. This soaks and further mixes the cap with the juice, extracting additional color and flavor.

There's no magic formula when it comes to how much maceration should take place, and the amount depends on the style of the wine. Wines without enough maceration will lack color, body, and structure, while those with too much are said to taste "over extracted," their texture and flavors coming across as too concentrated and aggressive.

A technique called carbonic maceration is sometimes used (notably in Beaujolais) for wines meant to be consumed young. In carbonic maceration, entire berries are placed in a closed vessel and topped with carbon dioxide. This environment creates a sort of mini-fermentation inside each berry, and the result emphasizes bright, candied, primary fruit flavors.

WHITE AND ROSÉ WINES

Fermentation for white and rosé wines usually takes place in steel vats (though wood is sometimes used for big-body white wines) and is deliberately kept cooler than the temperatures allowed for red wines. This elongates the fermentation process and allows more sediments to be extracted later.

Some white wines (famously, big, buttery Chardonnays) will then undergo malolactic fermentation, adding creamy notes and softer textures to the wine. It's common in many premium white wines (depending on the grape variety) for lees stirring (*bâtonage*) to take place. Lees are the dead yeast cells that precipitate out of the wine after fermentation and sometimes during aging. While it sounds unappealing, stirring the lees back into the wine periodically can imbue it with additional creaminess and add lovely brioche aromas.

SULFITES AND WINE

Poor sulfites . . . they are the pariahs of wine production. Sulfites in wine get bad press, but it might surprise you to learn that they're integral to wine chemistry and are used throughout the winemaking process. Without them, most wine would have a reduced shelf life (if not spoil entirely). Typically, white wines will have more sulfites than reds.

The reason that wine labels carry a sulfites warning is because about 1 percent of people have severe asthmatic allergic reactions to them; so no, they are probably *not* causing your headaches after drinking (too much) wine. For some perspective, dried fruit contains about five times the amount of sulfites that can be found in most bottles of white wine.

SPARKLING WINES

Now here is where winemaking gets really fun . . . and complicated.

Sparkling wines begin their lives as high-acid, low-alcohol "base" wines. These still base wines then undergo a secondary fermentation that will create all of those beguiling bubbles. Basically, there are two methods for doing this: fermenting a second time in the bottle or fermenting a second time in tanks.

The Champagne method (or *méthode traditionnelle*) is used to make Champagne, Cava, most of the Crémant sparkling wines throughout France, Franciacorta in Italy, and much of the best sparkling wine in the United States, Canada, Australia, Tasmania, and England. Using this method, the still base wines are bottled with a *liqueur de tirage*—a mixture of yeast and sugar—and sealed. Those bottles are then stored (either in cellars or air-conditioned storage areas), and the magic begins.

In each bottle, the yeast starts eating the sugar and another fermentation begins, but the resulting CO_2 has nowhere to go, so it gets absorbed into the wine. This gives the wine all of those lovely bubbles, while imparting texture, aroma, and flavor from the yeast cells. Next, the bottles are turned (or "riddled") either by hand on racks, or via an automated system called a gyropalette. This moves the sediment from this secondary fermentation into the neck of each bottle. Once this process is complete, the residue is disgorged from the neck of the bottle, and quickly replaced by a mixture of sugar and wine (called *liqueur d'expédition*), often a proprietary blend that determines the sweetness of the final wine. Finally, the bottle is corked, capped, and aged to let everything integrate.

Some sparkling wines such as Prosecco utilize the Charmat method, where secondary fermentation takes place in tank rather than in bottle. In this method, after the base wine is filtered, it's moved (under pressure) to another tank to undergo secondary fermentation, and the *liqueur d'expédition* is added before bottling. This is easier, quicker, and less expensive than the Champagne method, and produces fruitier wines that are meant to be enjoyed young.

In all cases, the bubbles and acidity in sparkling wine mitigate the wine's sense of sweetness, so even off-dry sparklers will feel relatively dry on your tongue (and drier versions will feel *very* dry).

Modern ingenuity meets the ancient technique of riddling: the gyropalette turns bottles of sparkling wine during their secondary fermentation.

Bubbles: From Budget to Big-Time

Sparkling wines come in many styles, and don't have to be pricey to be good. Here, we examine the range of sparkling wine, from everyday bubbles to world-class stunners.

La Marca Prosecco (Veneto, Italy)

Italian Prosecco is one of the most popular sparkling wine styles in the world, and this pale straw bubbly demonstrates why so many people love it. Made using the Charmat process to emphasize the grape's fruitiness, this example is light-bodied, lively with acidity, and full of green apple flavors and honeysuckle and citrus aromas.

Segura Viudas Brut (Cava, Spain)

Spanish Cava takes Champagne's production methods and uses them on grapes from the Catalan region (Macabeo, Parellada, and Xarel-lo). The result is an affordable, light bronze luxury that offers hints of almonds and toast (from aging on the lees), along with flavors of crisp apples (from the grapes).

Langlois Château Crémant de Loire Brut Rosé (Loire Valley, France)

Only first press (cuvée) juice from Cabernet Franc and Pinot Noir grapes grown in France's Saumur region are used to make this traditional-method sparkling rosé. It's a vibrant red bubbly blend that evokes aromas of tangy berries, oranges, and rose petals, while offering a delicate palate with red apple flavors and hints of toast.

Gloria Ferrer Blanc de Blancs (Carneros, California)

Blanc de Blancs are made entirely from white grapes (in this case, Chardonnay). Pale golden lemon hues in the glass are matched by lemon aromas, with a zestiness on the palate that moves to a slight creaminess as it finishes (a result of Chardonnay and yeast contact).

Laurent-Perrier Brut L-P (Champagne, France)

Laurent-Perrier's house style uses all three of Champagne's blending grapes (Chardonnay, Pinot Noir, and Pinot Meunier) and has an elegant palate. This is a great starting point for a foray into more expensive sparkling wines from the world's best bubbles region. The palate is as light, clean, vibrant, and refined as its pale golden color. Notes of citrus, brioche, and toast are followed by flavors of lemon zest and pear, finishing with a hint of smoke.

DESSERT AND FORTIFIED WINES

Most dessert wines are made from overripe grapes, which have been left on the vine longer (called "late harvest" or *spätlese* in German) to accumulate more sugars. Sometimes, they are left until they dry to raisins on the vine, or are dried into raisins after harvest, to further concentrate their sugars. In the winery, the yeasts don't convert all the extra sugars into alcohol, so the wine ends up with more sweetness and viscosity. Late harvest wines can be abundantly fruity, with candied aromas, and a lusciously sweet palate (thanks to also being lower in acidity).

Fortified wines (not all of which are meant for dessert) are another animal entirely. These are wines with serious attitude and usually clock in at 20 percent alcohol by volume. Examples include Rutherglen Muscat (from Australia), Port and Madeira (from Portugal), Sherry (from Spain), Marsala (from Sicily), and Banyuls and Rivesaltes (from France). There are two basic fortification methods: adding alcohol *during* fermentation or adding it *after* fermentation.

Most fortified wines (including Port and Madeira) are made by arresting the fermentation process. This is done by adding a neutral spirit (usually distilled from grapes) during fermentation. The spirit is so high in alcohol that it kills off the yeasts, stopping fermentation and preserving some of the wine's natural sugars (and substantially raising the wine's final alcohol level). This impacts the wine's sweetness (adding syrupy notes), body (making it fuller), and texture (adding roundness), while preserving aromatic complexity.

In the case of Sherry, the base wine completes fermentation and is put into partially filled barrels where a type of yeast called *flor* creates a cap on the wine, shielding it from exposure to oxygen. Grape brandy is added after fermentation, to fortify the final wine and create the various styles of drier or sweeter Sherry.

Fortified Wines: A Tasting Tutorial

Here are a few classic examples, from dry to sweet, that marry power with poise.

Osborne Manzanilla Sherry (Jerez, Spain)

Spanish Sherry on the drier side can be intriguing, like Osborne's pale bronze Manzanilla-style Sherry. Chamomile (Manzanilla means "chamomile infusion") and saline (imparted by its proximity to the sea) are the style's trademark aromas and here combine with vanilla and minerals. A powerful palate is topped off with rich flavors of baked green apples and almonds, which develop during barrel aging.

Graham's Six Grapes Reserve Port (Porto, Portugal)

Taking its name from Graham's six grapes symbol (once used to identify its best wine lots in the cellar), this is a great introduction to the fruit-forward Ruby Port style (which sees only a small amount of wood aging; if you like this one, start exploring more expensive vintage Ports). Opaque bluish-purple in the glass, this is opulent, full-bodied stuff, with blackberry and spice aromas, and rich plum (from the grapes) and rum (from the fortification) flavors.

Dow's Fine Tawny Port (Porto, Portugal)

This is bronzed brown in the glass, an effect of the style's extended wood aging and deliberate oxidation. It is big-boned, with caramel and pecan aromas, and hints of dried fruits (in contrast to the fresher fruits of the Ruby Port above).

Sandeman Fine Rich Madeira (Madeira, Portugal)

Dark amber in the glass, this is on the sweeter end for Madeira and is a good choice to pair with chocolate dessert. There are toast and wood notes from time spent in estufa (a type of oven that deliberately heats the wine, adding notes of baked fruit and spices), and the body is rich and powerful. Its concentrated fig and date flavors are carried on a nice line of acidity that cuts through the sweetness.

Cantine Florio Marsala Fine Sweet (Sicily, Italy)

Sicily's Marsala has a reputation for forgettable cooking wine, but their deep, dark amber fortified digestivo wines (which get their color from the use of cooked grape must) have much more to offer. Take this heady example from Cantine Florio: the fortification and winemaking processes impart caramel and brown sugar aromas, leading to flavors of stewed and spiced fruits, and a sweet, unctuous palate.

Maturation

Aging a wine evokes a certain sense of romance—who doesn't like visiting a charming, backlit cellar packed full of oak barrels, with a wine glass in hand? But there's more to it than putting a vintage away in storage for a few months. Maturing has a practical element: it clarifies wines.

In racking, wine is separated from the lees (dead yeast) and sediment by pouring it from one container (usually an oak barrel or steel tank) into another. This process clarifies the wine, exposes the wine to air briefly (which can soften its texture), and releases some of the CO_2 left from fermentation.

TO AGE OR NOT TO AGE

Usually a wine will only be aged when a) it has to be, by law, b) when the producer thinks that the wine will improve with exposure to oxygen, wood, and/or settling time, or c) to achieve a particular style (such as with Port, Sherry, and Madeira). Some white wines might also be aged on the lees left over from fermentation (in which case it's said to be aged *sur lie*) to impart additional creaminess to the texture and add notes of yeast, bread, and yogurt to the wine. High-end sparkling wines are often aged so that the carbonation and yeasty elements have time to integrate.

Many European wine regions (especially in Spain, France, Italy, and Portugal) set minimum requirements for maturing wine in barrel and in bottle (and producers often exceed these minimums). Most everyday wine, however, isn't aged, or is only aged for very brief periods so that they can be racked and filtered. Premium wines are often aged for much longer periods, anywhere from several months to a few years. In some cases, like Port and Madeira, wines can be aged in wood for decades.

Barrel Aging

Wines are aged in more types of vessels than you might imagine, from old clay amphorae to concrete. But wood barrel aging is the most common form of maturation for premium red wines, and also some white wines. (Aromatic white wines, delicate wines, and rosés almost never see any time in oak, as it would overpower their primary aromas and flavors.) Barrels come in many sizes, from 30-gallon *demi-barrique* half-barrels to centuries-old, enormous *foudre* casks that can hold hundreds of gallons of wine, large enough that an adult can climb inside.

Barrels of Flavor: The Influence of Oak

Fermenting and aging wine in wood barrels can have a profound impact on how that wine will eventually taste, smell, and feel in your mouth. In this tasting, we'll compare and contrast two sets of wines—one white and one red—with and without wood influence, so that you can experience those differences directly.

Jean-Marc Brocard Domaine Sainte Claire Petit Chablis (Burgundy, France)
Burgundy's Petit Chablis appellation offers a mid-priced entry point into how Chardonnay is done in the Chablis region: steely and pure, without touching oak. Lemon yellow in the glass, with a light body, pithy texture, and fine acidity, you'll find aromas of lemon peel and mineral, with grapefruit and fresh lemon flavors. What you won't find, however, is any trace of wood influence.

Rodney Strong 'Tri-County' Chardonnay (California)
Blended from grapes grown across three California winemaking counties, this Chardonnay is quite different from the Chablis. Sixty percent of this wine is barrel fermented, and it is aged for six months in oak (with lees stirring to add textural creaminess). Golden in color, with lemon curd and yellow apple notes, you'll find tropical fruit flavors on a broad palate. You will also pick up several oak nuances, from a smoother texture in the mouth to aromas of toast, vanilla, and baking spices.

G. D. Vajra Dolcetto d'Alba (Piedmont, Italy)
This red from one of Piedmont's best producers is aged only in stainless steel, so it doesn't get the oak treatment. Bright purple hues mark this grape variety, as does the combination of sour cherries, bramble, and violet aromas. The medium-bodied palate is soft and inviting, with cherry flavors and bouncy acidity—all shining through without any wood adornment.

Trapiche Oak Cask Malbec (Mendoza, Argentina)
This plummy, deep red-violet Malbec spends nine months aging in oak casks (hence its name). It presents a rich, full-bodied mouthfeel with power and grip, aromas of dried herbs, toast, and cedar, and dark cherry flavors that finish with vanilla, spices, and earthy mushroom—almost all of which comes from the time that the wine spends in oak.

The most common size is the Bordelaise barrel, holding about 60 gallons, produced by coopers specifically for aging wine. Oak from Slovenia, France, America, and Hungary is most often used, though sometimes other woods (like acacia and chestnut) are employed.

The interiors of wine barrels are "toasted" (or charred) to different levels prior to use, offering winemakers options for adding flavor to their wood-aged wines. A light toast only slightly changes the wood's color and can add notes of caramel, clove, and vanilla. A medium barrel toast browns the wood, adding bolder notes of cedar, coffee, and roasted nuts. Heavy toast barrels are noticeably darker in color and impart aromas and flavors of charcoal and baking spices (like cinnamon, ginger, and nutmeg).

The provenance of the wood, the amount of toasting, the wood grain, and the age of the barrel all play a part in the flavors and aromas imparted to the resulting wine. French oak adds spice and toast aromas, while American oak is bolder, supplying coconut and caramel notes. Older oak barrels have a lesser impact than newer barrels.

Size matters when it comes to barrel aging. Smaller barrels provide more contact between the wine and the wood, so the oak's impacts on flavor and texture will be amplified. Larger barrels reduce the ratio and the effects.

Wine barrels receive different levels of toasting, which impacts wine flavor.

Eight Wines Meant to Be Enjoyed Young

It's often joked that most wine is meant to be aged only for the amount of time that it takes you to safely drive it home from the local wine shop. The majority of wines produced today aren't meant for your cellar; they're crafted for immediate enjoyment (within twelve months of purchase). Thankfully, there's never been a better time to explore wines meant to be consumed young, with more varieties, styles, and higher quality available at lower price points than ever before. Here are eight wines for which a *lack* of patience is a virtue.

Zonin Prosecco Cuvée 1821 (Veneto, Italy)

Zonin is Italy's largest privately held wine company, crafting instantly likable and easily drinkable bubbly Prosecco from their estate plantings of Glera grapes. The Charmat method is used (where the secondary fermentation that adds the bubbles takes place in steel tanks), emphasizing youthful fruitiness. This is welcoming, friendly stuff from its golden-white, effervescent appearance to its floral, citric, and nutty aromas. It's light, off-dry, and best drunk while it's fresh and full of friendly, energetic acidity.

Chateau Ste. Michelle Gewürztraminer (Columbia Valley, Washington State)

Almost bronze in the glass, this easy-to-like (though difficult to pronounce) white is all about instant gratification. It starts with the grape's telltale aromas of flowers, cloves, and lychee, then offers pear flavors and feels generous and—thanks to Washington State's high amounts of sunshine, which promotes full grape ripeness—lush in the mouth. A hint of sweetness, combined with its spicy character, make it a great young sipper (and a nice match for Thai takeout).

Yalumba 'Y Series' Viognier (South Australia)

Some Viognier is meant for long-haul bottle aging. Others, like the "Y Series" from Australia's dependable producer Yalumba, are simply meant to add a bit of elegance to a Tuesday night. It's a vibrant straw color in the glass with hints of orange blossom, ginger, melons, and white figs on a rich palate that ends with cream and toast notes.

Banfi Rosa Regale Brachetto d'Acqui (Piedmont, Italy)

This slightly bubbly (frizzante), northern Italian classic (made from the fruity and fun Brachetto grape in Italy's northern Piedmont area) is best described as an instant party in a glass. If one glance at its vibrant cranberry color doesn't get your party groove on, a sniff of its fresh red berries and rose petal aromas will. In the mouth, there's light effervescence, sweet raspberry flavors, and an electric acidity with a dry finish.

Georges Duboeuf Beaujolais Nouveau (Beaujolais, France)

If ever there was a wine for "now," Beaujolais Nouveau is it. Made from Gamay grapes grown near Burgundy, it is meant to celebrate the first wine of the vintage and is specifically crafted to be enjoyed immediately upon release. Produced using a fruit-forward technique called carbonic maceration, these are purple-tinged red wines that are fresh and vibrant, with red berry flavors and hints of bubblegum sweetness. Gamay is naturally low in tannins, which means that this easy-drinking red will play nicely with various cuisines at nearly any dinner table.

Bogle Vineyards Old Vine California Zinfandel (California)

Here's a great example of getting a lot without spending a lot. Made from dry-farmed (nonirrigated) vines that average 60 to 80 years old, and aged for one year in American oak, Bogle's Zinfandel offers a great value. Its deep red hues and aromas of pepper, black raspberry, and vanilla (courtesy of the oak) are best enjoyed when this wine is young and while the palate is still strong, assertive, and fruity.

Catena 'Alamos' Malbec (Mendoza, Argentina)

Argentina's low costs of production can offer significant bang for the buck, like this entry-level Malbec made from Catena's high-altitude vineyards, which is crafted in a youthful, accessible style. Opaque in the glass, you'll get baking spices, ripe plums, and a hint of violets on the nose. Strong body and structure make it a good pick for steaks or burgers.

Bottle Aging

Once bottled, some wines are aged for an additional period, either because they will benefit from some time to let all of their elements coalesce and harmonize, or because they are required to by law, or both.

Most wines need to be clear and chemically stable when bottled, so sulfite is usually added at this step. Bottling is tricky and best left to bottling machines, to ensure that the wine gets the right temperature and minimal oxygen exposure to maximize its chances of getting to your store shelf safe and sound.

The more complex and age-worthy the wine, the more it will benefit from time in the bottle before release. This gives a wine time for its various elements—aromatic compounds, tannins, acids, sugars, preservatives, etc.—to begin to integrate and chemically stabilize. Additionally, for deeply tannic reds, this allows some softening of the tannins before the wine is released.

An automated bottling line puts on the finishing touches
before the bottles leave the winery.

Blending

Blending is the craft of mixing different elements—like grape varieties, vineyards, or finished lots of wine—into a particular style of wine with flavors, textures, or aromas that couldn't be achieved otherwise.

Most wines are blends. In fact, the benchmark wines of the world—from Champagne to Bordeaux to Châteauneuf-du-Pape to Port—are all blends. Even varietal wines usually have small percentages of other grapes in them or are blended from different vineyard plots of the same grape variety. Sometimes, a final blend is determined by the vineyard; such "field blends" happen when different grapes are planted, harvested, and vinified together. Usually, though, wines will finish vinification before being blended.

During vinification and the aging process, wines are tasted at multiple points to determine how they are progressing. In the case of varietal wines, different barrels or tanks might present different expressions of flavor, aroma, and texture, and so offer choices for the winemaker on how they will finally be assembled into a finished wine before bottling.

In other cases, wines made from multiple grape varieties are used: some for color; some for texture, structure, and mouthfeel; some for aromatic complexity; others for acidity; and still others for flavors. The final blend is often the result of multiple tasting efforts involving several winemaking staff members. While some regions regulate portions of the blending process (including what grapes are permitted), there are usually no hard-and-fast blending rules, and determining a final blend is closer to art than to science.

Blending can happen at nearly any point in the vinification process, but most typically takes place before a wine is aged or after aging and before bottling. Sometimes, several blending steps are employed. The aim of blending is to create something that is greater than the sum of its parts. Speaking from personal experience, I have taken many impeccably vinified lots of wine and blended them into a horrendous mess that no one would ever want to have pass their lips. For this reason, I greatly admire the wine professionals who are able to do this step well!

Ten Great Wine Blends

The best way to get a feel for the power of blending in winemaking is, of course, to taste some blended wines. Blending isn't just about matching different grape varieties, however. It can also combine fruit from different sources or put seemingly unrelated grapes together in ways that work wonders. Here are ten wines that showcase the art of blending.

D'Arenberg 'The Stump Jump' White (McLaren Vale, Australia)
An interesting blend of two white grapes that are often found together—Marsanne and Roussanne—with two that aren't, Sauvignon Blanc and Riesling. The result is an instantly interesting, pale-yellow, highly aromatic grab bag of floral notes and zesty grapefruit flavors.

Famille Perrin 'Famille du Rhône' Réserve White (Côtes du Rhône, France)
Rhône Valley is famous for its blends, and this one really shows how separate parts can make a tasty whole. Four traditional grapes of the region are combined here to make a yellow-gold wine with Viognier's white flower aromas, Grenache Blanc's round mouthfeel, and the tropical fruit and citrus flavors of Marsanne and Roussanne.

Moët & Chandon Brut Impérial (Champagne, France)
This famous Champagne house's Brut bubbly not only blends the region's three traditional grapes (Pinot Noir, Pinot Meunier, and Chardonnay), it also blends in more than 100 different wines from its inventory (called "library wines," about 25 percent of which are from older vintages). As a result, this light-gold Champagne feels rich in the mouth, with toast, baked apple, and brioche aromas and flavors.

Chateau d'Esclans 'Whispering Angel' Rosé (Côtes de Provence, France)
Most Provençal pinks are blended from different grapes. Here, the traditional red mix of Grenache, Cinsault, Carignan, and Syrah provide a salmon color, rose petal aromas, and red berry flavors, while the addition of the white Vermentino brings acidity and aromatic lift.

M. Chapoutier 'Belleruche' Rouge (Côtes du Rhône, France)
Rhône reds are usually blended affairs. In this case, the recipe is simple: Grenache for body, spice, and power, and Syrah for pepper aromatics, a deep red color, and juicy red fruit flavors.

Bogle Vineyards Old Vine Essential Red (California)
Petite Sirah, Syrah, and Zinfandel, sourced from older California vines, are aged in American oak to produce this deep garnet bargain pick. It has Zin's body and spice, with Syrah's approachable softness, and Petite Sirah's plummy flavors, and finishes it all with coconut and cedar oak notes.

Esporao Colheita Tinto (Alentejo, Portugal)
The Alentejo's largest producer blends Portugal's native Touriga Nacional with Spain's Aragonez (Tempranillo) and France's Cabernet Sauvignon, all grown in their organic vineyards. Spicy, bold, and fruity, this dark ruby red uses that interesting blend to combine Touriga's violet aromas, Tempranillo's tobacco notes, and Cabernet's red and black currant flavors.

Château Greysac Médoc (Bordeaux, France)
Predominantly Merlot and Cabernet Sauvignon, with small amounts of Cabernet Franc and Petit Verdot, this is classic stuff that won't break the bank. Garnet in the glass, you'll get currant and red berry flavors (from the Merlot), hints of spices and herbs (from the Cabernet), and a balanced palate weight (from the combination of both varieties). This is a great introduction to why Bordeaux is the master of the red blend, as the whole exceeds the sum of its parts.

Chateau Ste. Michelle Indian Wells Red Blend (Columbia Valley, Washington State)
Washington State struts its stuff with this blend, which combines not only several grapes (Syrah, Merlot, Malbec, Grenache, Cabernet Sauvignon, Cabernet Franc, Cinsault, Barbera, and Mourvèdre), but blends them from across several subregions of the Columbia Valley, too. The result is a wine with a big body (from the Grenache and Malbec), balanced acidity (from the Cinsault), big red and black fruit flavors, and plenty of baking spice notes (from everything else).

Dry Creek Vineyard Meritage Red Blend (Sonoma County, California)
"Meritage" is the term used for American-made reds that blend Bordeaux's grapes: Merlot, Cabernet Franc, Malbec, Petit Verdot, and Cabernet Sauvignon. Here, the Cabernet Franc and Petit Verdot provide the dried herb and violet notes and deep garnet color, while the Merlot, Malbec, and Cabernet Sauvignon add the full body and plum, cassis, and cocoa flavors.

Filtering/Fining

Once a wine is deemed ready, it can be filtered and bottled. Filtering has two main purposes: to further clarify the wine (so it's more aesthetically pleasing) and to further stabilize it (by removing unwanted microbes). If done correctly, this step can soften a wine's mouthfeel. If done incorrectly, filtering can deaden the wine's aromas and flavors.

A process called fining is used to help clarify wines in the cellar. During fining, small, unwanted particles (called colloids) are removed by binding them to some other element, so that they become large enough to more easily filter out before bottling.

There are many fining agents used in winemaking and, fair warning, they don't sound appetizing. The most common agents are bentonite (a type of clay, long used in traditional natural remedies), carbon, casein (milk-based proteins), egg whites, gelatin (from animal collagen), and isinglass (a jelly-like substance obtained from fish). Some of these fining agents can prevent a wine from being considered vegan, since they're derived from animals.

Fining is an important step for many wines but can sometimes suppress flavor and change the wine's texture. Therefore, some winemakers avoid fining or filtering their high-end wines (especially reds), in order to preserve as many of the original flavors and textures as possible. Typically, all wine will be fined and/or filtered unless it specifically mentions that it is unfined or unfiltered on the label. If you're in search of vegan wines, look for those that indicate that they are unfined.

The Final Product

Assuming all goes well, you now have a bottled wine, ready to ship, sell, or be given to critics like me for review (hey, I never said my job wasn't awesome!). But what's in the final product, and how does that impact taste?

ALCOHOLIC CONTENT

Wine is about 85 percent water, with the rest being made up of alcohol and volatile flavor and aroma compounds. It's in that 15 percent that the magic happens.

Non-fortified dessert wines, off-dry wines, and sparkling wines tend to have lower alcohol content, normally between 8 and 11 percent abv (alcohol by volume). Dry white and red wines run anywhere from 12 to 16 percent, and fortified wines reach about 20 percent.

Aside from adding a sense of body and palate weight to the finished wine, alcohol has a direct impact on how flavors and aromas are perceived, so that final number is important (and not just for knowing how loopy a wine can get you if you drink too much of it). The reason for this brings us back to chemistry.

Different aroma molecules act differently in various liquids based on how those molecules are structured. Some molecules (called hydrophobic) don't take well to water and so release into the air rather quickly when water is around (and therefore are easier for us to detect). Others have an affinity for water (hydrophilic) and it will be harder to get them to release their grip, making them more difficult to smell.

NATURAL AND ORANGE WINES

Both natural and orange wines (which are not the same thing) have been seeing increased popularity and media coverage, so chances are good that you'll encounter them at some point on your wine journey. Here's a quick primer on both:

Natural wine is a bit of a misnomer, as there isn't a formal definition for it. It can more accurately be described as a global movement among like-minded winemakers who are against crafting their wines with too many additives (such as sulfites) during the winemaking process, feeling that these can detract from the wine's natural expression. Often, their wines are not fined or filtered before bottling. Natural wines can be thought of as wines with minimal intervention, which requires more winemaking care, as it increases the potential for the wine to spoil from bacteria.

Orange wine is actually orange in color and can be thought of as a modern take on ancient winemaking techniques from Slovenia and northern Italy. These wines are made from white grapes that are left in contact with their skins (just as is done when making red wines), which imparts additional tannins, flavors, and structure, along with a deep amber hue. Orange wines are often unfined and unfiltered and can even be cloudy. While they are an acquired taste due to their additional structural bitterness, they can be fascinating to sip when made well.

The higher the alcohol level, the more hydrophilic aroma molecules you'll pick up (and vice versa for lower abv wines, which have a higher proportion of water by volume). This doesn't mean that higher alcohol wines are better, but it does mean that a wine with a higher abv percentage will smell and taste differently from one with a lower abv, even when made from the same grape varieties.

We also experience alcohol in wine's mouthfeel and body. Even powerfully alcoholic wines can (and should) feel somewhat balanced in the mouth. Be on the lookout for wines that feel too thin on the palate or seem too "hot" and boozy in the mouth; both mean that the wine is not completely in balance when it comes to the interplay of its sugars, acids, and alcohol content. Higher abv wines should seem rich and full, without being overbearing (or feeling like you're drinking a shot of jet fuel). Wines with less alcohol should have a lighter mouthfeel that can still be round, or emphasizes the wine's zesty characteristics, based on its acidity levels.

Tasting Notes Related to How a Wine Is Made

Here's a quick look at some of the aromas, flavors, and textures imparted during various stages of the winemaking process. This isn't exhaustive, but it will help you get your head around what you're smelling and tasting.

SOURCE	AROMAS	FLAVORS/TEXTURE
Malolactic fermentation	Cream, butter	Butter, yogurt Silky, smooth
Yeast	Brioche, toast, bread	Toast, baked bread, cream Roundness
Oak aging	Cedar, sandalwood, coconut, caramel, hazelnut, cloves, baking spices, cinnamon, vanilla, coffee, cocoa, toast, licorice	Coconut, tea (tannin), toffee, toast, licorice Leathery, grippy
Bottle aging–white wine	Honey, toasted nuts, dried fruits, earth	Dried fruits, toast Toasty, with a broad, soft palate
Bottle aging–red wine	Forest floor, mushrooms, chocolate, leather, game meat, walnut	Truffle, cocoa, smoked meat Softer, more supple palate

ACIDITY

We can't talk about a wine's acids without mentioning one of wine's most controversial topics: minerality.

In some wine regions (particularly in France), minerality is synonymous with acidity. Wine lovers, critics, and many New World winemakers will tell you, however, that they are not the same thing. Minerality is tricky because we don't know exactly *why* some wines have aromas and flavors that we associate with wet river stones, slate, chalk, flint, saline, or the like. We do know, however, that these elements are almost never picked up in wines with high pH (alkaline) levels, and so higher acid levels are necessary for mineral characteristics to be perceived in a wine. This explains why higher-acid white wines are more commonly described as being mineral than are lower-acid reds.

Perhaps more important, acidity plays a large role in how a wine's palate balance and weight are perceived. Acidity makes wines feel drier, so a wine that is very high in acids might need some residual sugar in order to feel more balanced in the mouth. Not enough acid and the wine will feel flat; too much and it will be searing to your tongue and gums (like sucking on a lemon). The right amounts are a matter of preference but even highly acidic wines should feel zesty and alive in the mouth in pleasant ways, exciting your salivary glands and refreshing your palate.

TANNIN CONTENT

Astringent tannins from grape skins and oak aging give structure to a wine. Some drinkers can handle more astringency than others. If you like your tea strong, chances are good that you will have a higher tolerance for the mouth-puckering sensation that tannic wines can bring. Just as with acidity, the "right" amount of tannins is a matter of style and preference. Even highly tannic wines can feel balanced, if the tannins are integrated well enough into the wine. In those cases, you should feel a sense of structure and power without also feeling like your mouth caught the wrong side of a cheese grater.

Tannins play important roles in both a wine's texture and its aging curve. I like to think of them as the scaffolding upon which the rest of the wine is constructed; without enough tannins, the wine will fall flat in your mouth. Too much and you've got yourself an overly austere construction that feels unfinished (not to mention being kind of painful to drink). Tannins are essential for red wines that are expected to age, so some young reds that aren't meant for immediate drinking will feel closed off and brutish in their youth, only to soften miraculously after those tannins precipitate during time in the bottle.

Watch out for a sensation of "greenness" or intense bitterness in a wine's tannins; those tend to come from too much contact with stems and seeds, and almost never age gracefully (we critics, in trying to be kind, might say that particular wine is too "rustic"). A wine might be low or high in tannins, but in both cases the tannic bite should feel part of an integrated whole.

BODY

All of the above elements come together to form what we call the wine's "body." By body, we mean the combination of a wine's texture and its weight in the mouth. Again, preference and style trump all, but the end result should feel in balance within that style. In other words, a wine can be smooth (in its tannins) and soft (in its alcohol) without feeling flabby (thanks to its acidity). Sure, one element might be more pronounced than another, but they should all be in service to wine's fundamental purpose in life, which is to bring pleasure.

You can think of a wine's body like a triangle with alcohol, acid, and tannin as its three corners. Each of these elements—resulting from choices made throughout the winemaking process—has a sizable impact on how the others are perceived. Move one angle, and the entire triangle can dramatically change shape. A well-balanced wine can (and should) have a unique "triangle" with its own particular characteristics, each contributing to the whole.

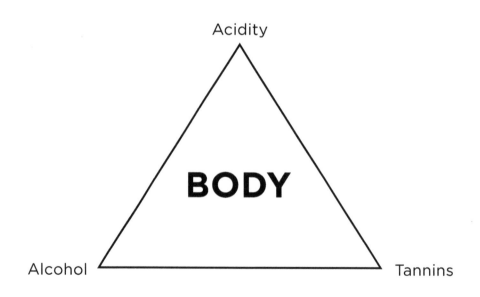

It's in the Making

This tasting is about the differences that vinification decisions can have on the wine that eventually graces your glass. Here, we'll explore how winemaking techniques can change the flavors, texture, and aromas of wine.

A to Z Wineworks 'Bubbles' (Oregon, USA)

This pale pink, incredibly fun sparkling rosé is made with Pinot Noir and Chardonnay grapes that spend small amounts of time in contact with the grape skins, imparting just a bit of color. It's then fermented in stainless steel to retain its freshness (and to add the bubbles). Fruity flavors of watermelon, cherry, and nectarine and a vivacious mouthfeel make this bubbly incredibly easy to imbibe.

Vietti Cascinetta Moscato d'Asti (Piedmont, Italy)

Moscato d'Asti is made by deliberately stopping fermentation early, so that not all of the grapes' sugars are converted into alcohol by the yeasts. You'll get a nice hint of sweetness (mitigated on the light, soft palate by a slight fizziness) in this pale-yellow example from northern Italy. It's lovely and floral, with ginger and peach notes, and flavors of apricot.

Vignobles Lacheteau Sur Lie Muscadet Sèvre et Maine (Loire Valley, France)

Hailing from the far western end of France's long Loire River wine region, Muscadet white wine is usually light and fresh. In some cases, however, the winemakers let the wine rest on the dead fermentation yeasts (sur lie), adding notes of brioche and softening the palate with a hint of creaminess. In this white, there are lemon flavors to match its pale lemon color, and citrus pith aromas, with the delicate palate rounded out by the lees contact.

Monti Montepulciano d'Abruzzo (Abruzzo, Italy)

Some winemakers deliberately bottle their red wines without fining or filtering in order to preserve the primary flavors and aromas. Monti's Montepulciano is a lively and full-bodied red that's not fined or filtered (a rarity at its affordable price point). As a result, it's a deep red color in the glass, complex on the nose (with licorice and spice aromas), and there's an added sense of purity to its blackberry and dark cherry flavors.

continued »

« continued from page 93

Bolla Amarone della Valpolicella Classico (Valpolicella, Italy)

Amarone is a still red wine made from grapes deliberately dried into raisins that undergo cold maceration, with the resulting juice high in sugars and extract. When the sugars are fermented, it imparts a huge body, high alcohol, ample acidity, and a hint of ripe fruit sweetness (from a small amount of sugar that the yeasts don't convert into alcohol). Bolla's Amarone checks all of those boxes, with its inky garnet color hinting at its power. Ripe cherry flavors, along with jam notes, complement this red's wood spice aromas (it spends over two years aging in Slavonian oak casks). This one is a little pricey, but as an alternative you can substitute a "ripasso"-style red from the same region (Valpolicella); these are made by running the grape juice over the grape must from Amarone wines (or "repassing" the wine, hence the name). The ripasso process gives those red wines similar qualities to Amarone, but with a slightly lighter body.

La Playa Late Harvest Sauvignon Blanc (Colchagua Valley, Chile)

Late harvest dessert wines are named for their production technique: leaving grapes on the vine to over-ripen, thus concentrating their sugars and intensity. In turn, those grapes can be made into wines that retain sugar and offer expressions that are more concentrated than their dry-wine counterparts. Chile's La Playa makes a consistently delicious version from white Sauvignon Blanc grapes. It has a golden lemon color; honey, brown sugar, and mandarin aromas; and concentrated grapefruit and starfruit flavors. While definitely sweet and round in the mouth, it has a sense of buoyancy thanks to the grape's naturally high acidity.

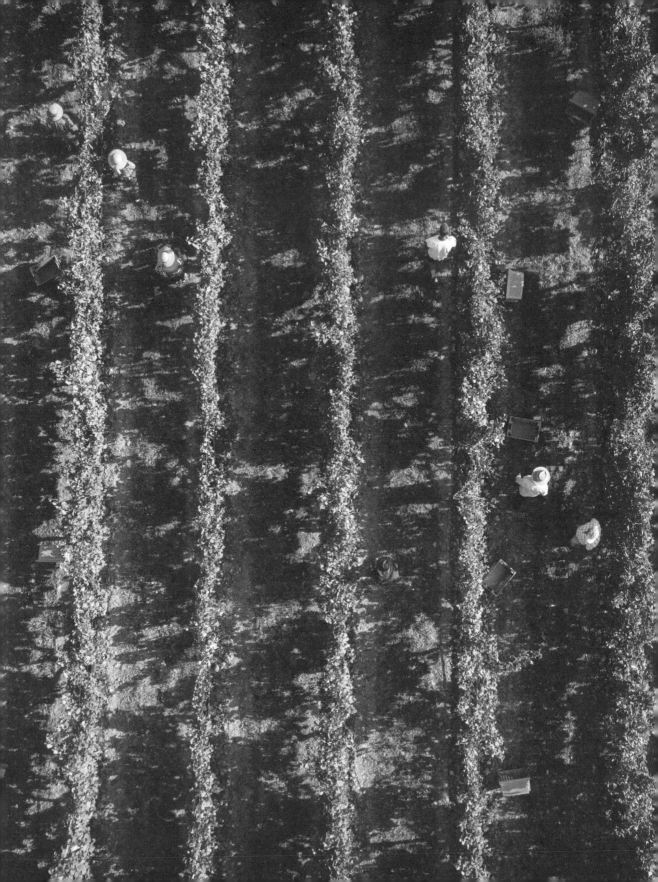

CHAPTER 4

THE WORLD'S MAJOR WINE REGIONS

In this chapter, you'll take a journey through the major wine-producing regions across the globe, discovering the wine styles that they make, why and how they make those wines, and what all of that ultimately means for the wine that ends up in your glass.

The winemaking countries in this chapter are the ones you're most likely to find on the retail shelf, listed in descending order of how much wine they produce. At the time of this writing, the top five wine-producing nations in the world are Italy (at number one), followed by France, Spain, the United States, and Argentina.

ITALY

Vine plantings move with the rolling hillsides in Italy's northern Langhe area.

MAJOR GRAPE VARIETIES: *White:* Arneis, Catarratto, Chardonnay, Fiano, Friulano, Garganega (for Soave), Glera (for Prosecco), Grechetto, Grillo, Malvasia, Moscato Blanc, Pinot Grigio, Riesling, Sauvignon Blanc, Trebbiano, Verdicchio, Vermentino, Vernaccia; *Red:* Aglianico, Barbera, Bonarda, Cabernet Sauvignon, Corvina (for Amarone), Dolcetto, Frappato, Lambrusco, Merlot, Montepulciano, Nebbiolo (for Barbaresco and Barolo), Negroamaro, Nero d'Avola, Pinot Nero, Primitivo, Refosco, Sagrantino, Sangiovese, Syrah, Teroldego

MAJOR WINES PRODUCED: Varietal and blended wines of all styles from indigenous and transplanted grape varieties, Amarone, Barbaresco, Barolo, Brunello di Montalcino, Chianti, Franciacorta, Lambrusco, Marsala, Moscato d'Asti, Prosecco, Soave, Valpolicella, Vino Nobile di Montepulciano

If it sometimes feels as though Italian wine is ubiquitous, that's because it is. Italy regularly vies against France and Spain as the world's highest volume wine producer each year, with about 1.5 million acres of grapes in cultivation. Italy makes 20 percent of all wine sold globally and has more native wine grape varieties than any other nation on Earth.

Italy's potential for excellent wine was obvious even in ancient times. Wine production in Italy began with the Etruscans and Greeks. The Romans later took winegrowing to a whole new level, significantly expanding plantings throughout what is now modern Italy. Today, Italy makes almost every conceivable type of wine, from lighter whites (like Soave) to off-dry spritzy delights (Moscato d'Asti) to full-throttle reds (Amarone) to succulent dessert wines (often from dried grapes, called *passito*).

Due to Italy's diverse winemaking techniques, grape varieties, traditions, regions, climates, and geography, it's impossible to describe a single style of Italian wine. I find it helpful to think of Italy in terms of two halves: the northern half has a cooler, more continental climate, while the southern half is more Mediterranean and warmer. This impacts the grapes grown and the possible styles of wine made. Here are some of the major regions within those halves, moving roughly from north to south, along with some of their most famous vinous specialties.

PIEDMONT

This hilly, northwest area might be Italy's most diverse wine region, and it has several appellations within it (many overlapping one another), all drastically different in style. With lots of sunlight and a cool growing season, many grape varieties thrive in Piedmont, retaining their energetic acidity even when fully ripened. The famously fun and fizzy Moscato d'Asti wines are made here, as is Barbera d'Asti, along with two of Italy's most long-lived and powerfully struc-tured reds, Barolo and Barbaresco (both from the Nebbiolo grape).

LOMBARDY

Lombardy sits in central northern Italy and has a cool continental climate influenced by both the Alps and the region's many picturesque lakes, includ-ing tourist-friendly Lake Garda, where age-worthy, energetic Lugana whites are made (from the Turbiana grape, a relative of Verdicchio). Lombardy's best-known vinous export, however, is Franciacorta, a sparkling wine that uses the same grapes and methods as Champagne (and can be just as good).

TRENTINO-ALTO ADIGE

This northern region is influenced by its proximity to Austria (two-thirds of Alto Adige still speaks German, where the area is called Südtirol, which some-times appears on wine labels), growing many white varieties that are rarities in the rest of Italy (such as Riesling). Pinot Grigio shines here, making zesty, refreshing whites. Because of its cooler climate, this mountainous area is also famous for traditional-method sparkling wines (especially in Trento DOC), often using the same grapes as Champagne.

FRIULI-VENEZIA GIULIA

Abutting mountains in Italy's northeast, Friuli-Venezia Giulia is known for high-acid wines that are lighter-bodied and livelier, and have more structure than their southern counterparts, with whites made from Friulano and Ribolla Gialla (particularly in the southern area of Collio), and reds from Cabernet Franc and Merlot.

VENETO

While cool, this northeastern region near Venice is protected from severe cold weather by the Alps. The Veneto produces several wine styles but is noted for four appellations in particular. First is Prosecco, the fruit-forward, fun sparkling wines made from the Glera grape variety. Next is Soave, a light- to medium-bodied, zesty, citric white made from Garganega. Finally, we have what are the polar opposites of those whites: Valpolicella and Amarone. Both are reds based on the Corvina variety, made using dried grapes that increase their spiciness, concentration, and alcoholic potency.

EMILIA-ROMAGNA

This northern region, near Bologna, is one of Italy's largest and most prolific wine areas. Most will recognize the name Lambrusco, a red berry–flavored, usually off-dry, semi-sparkling wine made from the red grape of the same name. Lambrusco can offer excellent value (and a lot of fun) for the money when it's made well.

TUSCANY

Tuscan wines are as famous as the area's beautiful, rolling landscape, and for good reason. This central region is the country's third-largest wine producer and home to Chianti as well as to full-bodied white wines and dessert-style Vin Santo. Sangiovese is the leading grape, making acid-driven, tangy, spicy, medium- to full-bodied reds. Many clonal variations of Sangiovese are used in Tuscany, one of which makes the dense, layered reds of Brunello di Montalcino. This region is also home to "Super Tuscan" reds: premium wines utilizing international varieties like Cabernet Sauvignon. By including varieties outside their regional regulations, these wines were forced to use "lower" quality tiers on their labels yet received rave reviews and commanded higher prices than supposedly superior DOC wines. Their success has forced regulation changes, with pioneering subregions such as Bolgheri qualifying as their own DOC wine.

UMBRIA

This area, which lacks a coastline, is situated to the south of Tuscany. While it is known for white wines made from both Trebbiano and Grechetto, its highest classifications are reserved for reds. The most notable is Sagrantino from the Montefalco area. Sagrantino reds are among the plummiest, most densely concentrated, tannic, and powerful of any in Italy. To tame its tannins, Sagrantino is often blended with other varieties (including Sangiovese) or aged for extended periods.

ABRUZZO

This eastern central region is mountainous, which limits its vineyard area. That hasn't stopped it from becoming one of the highest production regions in all of Italy, though. Its most famous red is made from the Montepulciano variety (not to be confused with the *village* of Montepulciano, in Tuscany), which ripens well in Abruzzo's warmer climate. These are hearty, almost jet-black wines that are moderate in acidity, but high in concentrated red and black fruit flavors. The tannins are ripe and soft, making these wines feel lush in the mouth.

CAMPANIA

If Italy is a boot, then Campania is its shin in the south. One of the oldest wine regions in Italy, it is sunny, warm, and dry, making it relatively easy to ripen grapes there. Campania makes fascinating whites (especially from Falanghina, Fiano, and Greco), but is best known for reds made from Aglianico. Aglianico wines have the volume turned up on acidity, tannin, body, and black cherry fruitiness.

PUGLIA

The "heel" of Italy's boot, Puglia enjoys a warm, moderate climate thanks to its long stretch of coastline along the Mediterranean. The region is best known for red wines made from Primitivo (aka Zinfandel). But Puglia also specializes in the versatile Negroamaro grape, capable of producing spicy red wines that evoke licorice, tobacco, and prunes (and also made into surprisingly fresh, floral rosés).

SARDINIA AND SICILY

Italy's two large islands have distinct wine cultures. The slightly smaller of the two, Sardinia, sits 150 miles west of Italy's coast. Due to its many cultural influences, it grows grapes that are rarely found on mainland Italy, such as Carignan and Cannonau (Grenache). Its highest classified wines are white, crafted from Vermentino, and are lively, with citrus flavors and notes of almonds and herbs.

Dominated by the still-active Mount Etna volcano, Sicily is the Mediterranean's largest island. It has been ruled by Arabs, Greeks, Phoenicians, and Italians, and this cultural blending pot is reflected in its diverse wine scene. You're most likely to encounter whites made from Grillo (medium-bodied, and delicious, with white peach flavors and white flower aromas), reds from Nero d'Avola (deeply colored, full-bodied, and full of spice and juicy plum flavors), and Marsala (figgy, nutty, rich fortified wines, ranging from dry/*secco* to sweet/*dolce*).

Tuscany is best known for its gorgeous hillside towns and delicious red wines.

A Tasting Tour: Northern Italy

Northern Italy contains some of the most famous and diverse wine regions in all of Europe. This tasting will give you a feeling for its vinous possibilities.

Ferrari Brut (Trento)

This yellow straw sparkler is made from Chardonnay grapes grown on the mountain slopes in Trentino-Alto Adige, using traditional Champagne methods. There are fine, persistent bubbles, with jasmine and yellow apple aromas, and a lighter-bodied palate bursting with apple and lemon flavors, with lots of acidity. It ends with hints of baked bread, from having aged on its yeast lees.

Cantina della Volta Lambrusco di Modena Spumante (Emilia-Romagna)

The Lambrusco grape hasn't always had the best reputation, but it can be really good, as in this bright pink, semi-sparkling example. Pomegranate, red berry, and rose petal aromas and raspberry flavors (coming directly from the grape when grown in cooler climates) make this bright on the palate and fun to drink.

Inama Vin Soave Classico (Veneto)

The white wines of Soave (made from Garganega grapes) are light in body, with jasmine, nut, and lemon-lime aromas and flavors, and the palate feels both refreshing and generous in its fruitiness.

Renato Ratti Barbera d'Asti (Piedmont)

Deep ruby-red, this is a full-bodied Barbera from the northern Italian region where it grows best. The aromas are of spices, violets, and black cherries, the flavors of wild, ripe raspberries, and the palate is rich without being overbearing. Through it all, the acidity of Barbera shines, making this wine feel energetic in the mouth.

Villadoria 'Bricco Magno' Langhe Nebbiolo (Piedmont)

Barolo and Barbaresco—the King and Queen of northern Italy's red wines—can be tannic monsters in their youth, making them difficult to taste while young. They are also expensive, so before you shell out for them, you need to be sure that you like the flavors supplied by the grape from which they're made: Nebbiolo. Fortunately, younger, less tannic (and more affordable) versions of Nebbiolo exist for us to try, like this one. Dark ruby with brick highlights, the wine opens with rose petal, vanilla, cedar, and dark chocolate aromas. Ripe red plum flavors dominate the palate, which is full and intense, thanks to Nebbiolo's high acidity and grippy tannins.

A Tasting Tour: Southern Italy

The southern half of Italy, with its Mediterranean climate, offers plenty of sunshine and warm temperatures for its grapes, which develop into ripe, rich wines. From the islands to Umbria, this tasting tour of Italy's south might have you reaching for your favorite Italian cookbook.

Cantine Argiolas 'Costamolino' Vermentino di Sardegna (Sardinia)

The lesser-known Vermentino might be Italy's sexiest secret-weapon white grape. Argiolas's version is a light-golden wine with pine, mint, and herbal notes along with lemon aromas. The palate is medium-bodied and fresh, with lingering stone and citrus flavors, and a perfect match for seafood (a classic pairing for this island wine).

Donnafugata 'SurSur' Grillo (Sicily)

Light-yellow in color, this wine is made from the Grillo grape and named after an Arabic term for the crickets that inhabit Sicily's vineyards. Wet stone, grass, and lemon peel aromas match a palate that's fresh and clean and has dangerously easy-to-drink tropical and citrus flavors.

Cantele Negroamaro Rosato (Puglia)

Negroamaro reds can be a tannic mouthful, but in this dry rosé version its wild nature is tamed. The wine is bright in all the right ways, from its almost ruby-red color to its aromas of dried rose petals and cherries to its fresh, lighter body and ripe red berry flavors.

Bisceglia 'Terre del Vulcano' (Campania)

From Campania's volcanic soils come the thick-skinned Aglianico grapes used to make this opaque, garnet-red wine. Blackberry, licorice, and violets are on the nose, with plum and dark cherry flavors in the mouth. While powerful, it's more medium-bodied, and the tannins feel round and smooth.

Arnaldo-Caprai Montefalco Rosso (Umbria)

This red is a blend of Sangiovese, Merlot, and Sagrantino (the Montefalco region's signature grape). It has plentiful wild red fruit, pepper, and dried herb aromas, dark plum flavors, and a full body. The toughness of Sagrantino's structure is held in check by the roundness of the Merlot and the acidity of the Sangiovese, making this a big wine that's easy to enjoy now.

FRANCE

Storybook beauty meets farming in France's Alsace wine region.

MAJOR GRAPE VARIETIES: *White:* Chardonnay, Chenin Blanc, Gewürztraminer, Marsanne, Muscat Blanc à Petits Grains, Riesling, Roussanne, Sauvignon Blanc, Sémillon, Viognier; *Red:* Cabernet Franc, Cabernet Sauvignon, Carignan, Cinsault, Gamay, Grenache, Malbec, Merlot, Mourvèdre, Pinot Meunier, Pinot Noir, Syrah

MAJOR WINES PRODUCED: Alsace varietal wines, Beaujolais, Bordeaux, Burgundy, Crémant de Loire, Champagne, Côtes du Rhône, Sauternes

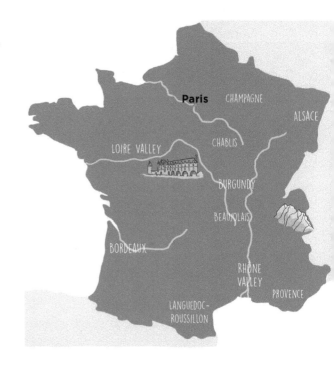

READING A FRENCH WINE LABEL

France's wine labels usually do not designate grape varieties, instead relying on the appellation to clue the consumer in to what grapes were used to make the wine. Some regions permit terms that designate the quality of the vineyard where the wine's grapes are harvested, but the terms don't always mean the same thing across regions.

Here are some of the more common terms you will find:

Appellation d'Origine Contrôlée (AOC or AC), or d'Origine Protégée (AOP): High-quality wine, from a region with strictest quality and control standards

Blanc: White wine

Château: Estate

Côte: Hillside

Cru: Exceptional vineyard (Alsace) or wine-growing village (Beaujolais)

Cru Bourgeois: Very good classified producer (St.-Émilion)

Cru Bourgeois Exceptionnel: Exceptional classified producer (St.-Émilion)

Cru Bourgeois Supérieur: Superior classified producer (St.-Émilion)

Cru Classé: Excellent producer (Provence)

Grand Cru: Exceptional, top-tier vineyard (Burgundy) or wine-growing village (Champagne)

Grand Cru Classé: Exceptional producer in Médoc, Graves, and Sauternes (ranked First through Fifth "growths" in 1855 classification)

Grand Vin: Meaning "great wine," an unregulated marketing term, like "Winemaker's Selection" in the United States

Millésime: Vintage

Premier Cru: Excellent, second-tier vineyard (Burgundy) or wine-growing village (Champagne)

Premier Grand Cru Classé: Exceptional producer (St.-Émilion)

Rouge: Red wine

Vieilles vignes: Old vines

Vigneron: Grape grower

Vin: Wine

Vin de Pays or Indication Géographique Protégée (IGP): Country wine

Vin de Table/Vin de France: Table wine

For many, France is synonymous with wine, not only because it's among the top three global producers by volume, with two million acres of grapes. It's also because, for many of the most famous wine grape varieties, a French region is considered its global benchmark wine, influencing how those varieties are grown in every other winemaking country. The best wines from the most historic French regions are coveted by collectors and demand some of the highest bottle prices in the world.

In France, the concept of *terroir* is woven inextricably into how its wine is produced, and with few exceptions, grape varieties are not printed on the label and must be inferred from their regional designation (causing no small amount of headaches for American shoppers). Not surprisingly, the current quality tier system used to regulate wine production throughout the European Union began in France.

Wine in France dates back over 2,500 years, likely starting with the Phoenicians in the 6th century BCE, with viticulture then being spread across the region by the Romans. Throughout its history, from the rise of trade with other European countries and the influence of the Catholic Church (which owned much vineyard land), wine has flourished in France. In the 1850s, France was ground zero for the phylloxera epidemic, caused by a louse (imported accidentally from America) that devastated much of Europe's vineyards. This is the reason that today, European grape varieties are grafted onto American vine rootstock, which is phylloxera-resistant, and is partly why French grape varieties proliferated throughout South America (as winegrowers fled the epidemic in search of work, bringing vine cuttings with them).

France's wine production is among the most varied and extensive of any country. Here's a primer on the French regions that you're most likely to encounter.

ALSACE

Bordered by the Vosges mountains, Alsace was once German and still carries influences from that country, including printing the grape variety on their wine labels. While many styles of wine (including sparkling and sweet) are made there, white wine production dominates in cooler-climate Alsace, making age-worthy, acid-driven wines primarily from Riesling, Pinot Gris, Pinot Blanc, and Gewürztraminer (for which it is the world standard).

BEAUJOLAIS

The home of the fruity, fun, but oft-maligned Beaujolais Nouveau, Gamay is the dominant grape grown in this cool region situated south of Burgundy in East-Central France. It's best known for light-bodied, low-tannin reds, often using carbonic maceration techniques during winemaking to emphasize Gamay's exuberant fruit aromas. The region's best wines (from ten *Cru* villages), however, can be high in both quality and longevity.

BORDEAUX

With almost 300,000 acres, 8,500 producers, 54 appellations, and a 700 million bottle-per-year output, Bordeaux is the largest thing going in French wine. Situated in the southwest, the area covers land around the Dordogne and Garonne rivers, which combine into the Gironde estuary. The storied producers located on the banks of the Gironde are why we sometimes refer to "Left Bank" (including Graves and Médoc, dominated by Cabernet Sauvignon) and "Right Bank" (most famously Saint-Émilion and Pomerol, dominated by Merlot) when talking about Bordeaux's reds.

Bordeaux is famous for its wine classification of 1855, commissioned by Emperor Napoleon III for the Exposition Universelle de Paris, which categorized the producers of red Médoc and sweet Sauternes-Barsac into five tiers, according to price. The concept stuck, and we still refer to some of the famous chateaus involved as First through Fifth "growths," with the top tiers producing some of the world's best red wines.

BURGUNDY

Located in Eastern France, the relatively cool area of Burgundy, with the Côte d'Or at its center, is the world standard-bearer for both Pinot Noir and Chardonnay. The best examples of each are made in tiny quantities and fetch exorbitant prices at auction. Burgundy's sub-appellations are famous, and its regional designations are more closely linked to *terroir* than anywhere else in France. Burgundy has five main regions (listed from north to south).

Chablis: Located in Northern Burgundy, this is the home of un-oaked Chardonnay, with crisp, acid-driven white wines with pure Chardonnay fruit expression being the norm.

Côte de Nuits: Production here is dominated by Pinot Noir, and it's home to Gevrey-Chambertin and the famous Vosne-Romanée, source of some of the world's most expensive red wines.

Côte de Beaune: Growing more Pinot Noir in the north, and more Chardonnay in the south, this region includes appellations such as Pommard, Volnay, Meursault, and Puligny-Montrachet.

Côte Chalonnaise: This is the main production area of Burgundy, most of it coming from the Mercurey appellation.

Mâconnais: This region produces mostly Chardonnay, including the famous Pouilly-Fuissé.

CHAMPAGNE

Champagne's name is so recognizable that it has become shorthand for sparkling wine globally. Located near Belgium, it's one of the coldest wine regions in France, dominated by chalky soils in which Romans dug mining caves (some still bearing the marks of the ancient tools used to create them), where most Champagne is aged. The area was known for still wine production since medieval times, and the "discovery" of sparkling wine likely happened accidentally, with vessels of unstable wines spontaneously undergoing secondary fermentation (and probably exploding). In the 1600s, glassmaking became reliable enough that the secondary fermentation that creates the bubbles could be done on purpose and stored safely.

Three grapes are used for Champagne blends (which can be white or rosé): red Pinot Meunier and Pinot Noir, and white Chardonnay. Styles are categorized according to the grapes used (Blanc de Blancs from Chardonnay, Blanc de Noirs from the red grapes only), and sweetness levels. Unless a vintage is specified, Champagne is usually a blend of multiple vintages, with major producers using the process to differentiate their "house" style.

READING A CHAMPAGNE LABEL

Champagne labels include style terms that clue you in to its potential sweetness level. Confusingly, many of the sweeter styles have the word *sec* ("dry") in their title. These regulated terms are, from driest to sweetest:

- Brut Nature
- Extra Brut Brut
- Extra-Sec

- Sec
- Demi-Sec
- Doux

There are also small initials on Champagne labels that indicate the type of producer:

NM: Négociant-Manipulant (they buy grapes and then make the Champagne)

RM: Récoltant Manipulant (grapes are grown and the wine made by the same producer, aka "Grower Champagne" or "Farmer Fizz")

CM: Coopérative de Manipulation (made by a collection of smaller growers)

RC: Récoltant-Coopérateur (made by a cooperative of growers, but under each grower's own branding)

SR: Société de Récoltants (grape growers share the same winery facilities, but make their own wines separately)

ND: Négociant Distributeur (they sell Champagne made by others)

MA: Marque d'Acheteur (a custom brand, such as those made for supermarket chains)

LANGUEDOC-ROUSSILLON

With fewer regulations than France's other wine regions, the southern, coastal Languedoc-Roussillon area is France's largest wine area by size and sees more innovative experimentation, growing grape varieties from throughout France (including Merlot, Cabernet Sauvignon, Mourvèdre, Grenache, Syrah, Viognier, and Sauvignon Blanc). This is an exciting region, with wines that tend to be rich and fuller-bodied and crafted in various styles, including sparkling (e.g., Crémant de Limoux) and sweet (such as Muscat de Rivesaltes).

LOIRE VALLEY

Spanning most of the 629-mile-long Loire River, the Loire Valley is a cool-climate region where location and vintage greatly influence the style and flavors of wines made in each of its 87 appellations. It's nearly as large as Bordeaux and, with its Crémant de Loire, is the second-largest sparkling wine producer in France after Champagne.

You could spend several tastings just scratching the surface of Loire's many appellations. It helps to think of the Loire in three sections, to get a handle on its size and vinous diversity:

Upper Loire: The far east of the region, it includes Sancerre and Pouilly-Fumé and is dominated by racy Sauvignon Blanc. Other varieties are grown there, too, like Pinot Noir for delicate red and rosé wines.

Middle Loire: This area includes Chinon, Touraine, Saumur, and Vouvray, primarily producing Cabernet Franc (for reds) and Chenin Blanc (for dry white, sweet, and sparkling wines).

Lower Loire: The western portion of the region, it extends to the Atlantic, producing the delicate, seafood-friendly Muscadet wine, made with Melon de Bourgogne.

PROVENCE

Located in the far southeast and enjoying a Mediterranean climate, Provence is the heart of France's dry rosé production. It's famous for rosés from Côtes de Provence, a large appellation covering over 80 communes in the eastern portion of the region. (The Bandol area, which produces red wines from Mourvèdre, is also well known.) Because of the powerful mistral winds in the area, farming techniques that avoid conventional chemicals are used.

RHÔNE VALLEY

Viticulture around the Rhône river in Southern France dates back to the 6th century BCE, but really took off in the 13th century when the papacy moved to Avignon. (This is the source of the Southern Rhône's most famous appellation's name, Châteauneuf-du-Pape, or "new castle of the pope.") Today, the area is a hotbed for full-bodied whites and big-boned red wines, much of it made under the Côtes du Rhône appellation. (Rosés and sparkling wines are made here, too.) The reds often carry an aroma of *garrigue*, a mixture of wild Mediterranean herbs like thyme, rosemary, and lavender.

There are two distinct portions to this region, which differ in climate and dominant grape varieties:

Northern Rhône: This area has a continental climate, with cold winters and warm summers, and sees influence from the strong mistral winds. Syrah is the dominant grape, making the peppery, sinewy red wines from appellations such as Côte-Rôtie, Hermitage, and Saint-Joseph. Floral white wines are made from Viognier in Condrieu and Château-Grillet, or from Marsanne and Roussanne in most of the other appellations.

Southern Rhône: This section of the valley is more Mediterranean in climate, experiences less influence from the mistral, and has several appellations among its varied microclimates. In many areas, large stones (somewhat inappropriately called *galets* or "pebbles") dominate the vineyards, absorbing heat from the sun and later releasing it onto the grapes. While rosé (most notably in Tavel) and fortified wines are made, the region is dominated by brambly, dense, and powerful reds, especially from Châteauneuf-du-Pape. These are blended from several varieties (Grenache, Syrah, Mourvèdre, Carignan, and Cinsault are most used). Southern Rhône's heady, rich white wines are blends, too, primarily of Roussanne, Bourboulenc, Picpoul, Clairette, and Ugni Blanc.

France's Cooler Side

France's cooler half is home to some of the most expressive wine regions in the world; this tasting will give you a quick tour without emptying your bank account. For further tastings of French wines, see *Shades of Gray: Pinot Gris/Grigio* (page 47), *Gamay Beyond Nouveau* (page 34), *Barrels of Flavor: The Influence of Oak* (page 80), *Bubbles: From Budget to Big-Time* (page 76), *Ten Great Wine Blends* (page 86), *Beyond Bordeaux: France's Famous Blending Grapes* (page 40), and *It's in the Making* (page 93).

Domaine des Côtes Blanches Sancerre (Loire Valley)
This straw-yellow, medium-bodied Sauvignon Blanc comes from the Eastern Loire and showcases the lighter style most common to the region. It has a delicate, acidic texture, light grapefruit flavors, and reserved aromas of lemon, hay, and flint.

Trimbach Riesling (Alsace)
This perennially excellent, green-tinged, straw-colored wine is the perfect ambassador for Alsatian-style Riesling. Spice, herbs, and ripe lemon aromas are followed by juicy stone fruit and ripe citrus flavors on a vibrant, fresh palate. It feels as tight as steel in the mouth with its high acidity but is also deliciously easy to drink.

Louis Jadot Mâcon-Villages (Burgundy)
Yellow apples, Meyer lemon, and honeydew melon greet you when you sniff this pale-gold Burgundy, made entirely from Chardonnay. The flavors mirror the nose, delivered with focus and purity on the medium-bodied palate, a result of the climate, which allows the grapes to ripen slowly and retain their natural acidity.

Barton & Guestier Vouvray (Loire Valley)
This is an affordable introduction to Vouvray, a Middle Loire region that specializes in Chenin Blanc. Clear yellow in the glass, this has a nose that's fruity (with pineapple and white peach) and mineral (like wet river stones), with a tropical fruit palate that's balanced between freshness and ripeness.

Joseph Drouhin Côte de Beaune Villages (Burgundy)
Drouhin manages to offer this Pinot Noir (sourced from villages on the Côte de Beaune) at a reasonable, mid-level price. The nose is classic cooler-climate Pinot, with delicate aromas of red berries, dried citrus peel, and spice. The palate changes things up, offering flavors of black fruits and raspberries that feel round and full.

France's Warmer Side

The southern half of France is sunnier, drier, and warmer than the northern half. This results in wines that favor red grapes and a riper style. In this tasting, we'll explore those sunnier French climes and the wines that they produce. For more southern French exploration, see *Ten Great Wine Blends* (page 86), *Think Pink: The Surprising Diversity of Rosé* (page 68), and *Wine + Food: Complement and Contrast* (page 176).

Domaines Barons de Rothschild 'Légende' Bordeaux Blanc (Bordeaux)
Almost equal parts Sauvignon Blanc and Sémillon, this white wine is fashioned in the classic Bordeaux Blanc style. Greenish-straw in the glass, it has acacia, graphite, white peach, and lemons on the nose, with a palate that is medium-bodied and full of ripe citrus and melon. Like many Bordeaux Blanc wines, it's reserved when young, sometimes needing a few months of bottle aging to open up fully.

Château Faizeau Montagne-St.-Emilion (Bordeaux)
Mostly Merlot, with some Cabernet Franc, this red is quintessential "Right Bank" Bordeaux. Ruby-colored with violet edges, there are black plum and black olive notes, and nice palate roundness from the Merlot. The structure and licorice spice from the Cabernet Franc add depth and dimension.

Paul Jaboulet Aîné 'Les Cyprès' Vacqueyras (Rhône Valley)
From a blend of traditional Southern Rhône red grapes comes this full-bodied, oak-aged, purple and garnet wine. Made in a similar style to the much more expensive reds of nearby Châteauneuf-du-Pape, Vacqueyras can offer real bargains. Here, we find leather, rosemary, and dark cherry aromas, with wood spice notes from its time in oak. The tannins feel well integrated, offering a smooth, lush palate of ripe black fruits and red plum flavors.

M. Chapoutier 'Les Vignes de Bila-Haut' Côtes du Roussillon Villages (Languedoc-Roussillon)
This Grenache, Syrah, and Carignan blend comes from the slopes of the Agly Valley in the south of France, and sees no oak aging, so we get the pure fruit expression of the grapes themselves. Full-bodied and opaque purple, it's a densely packed wine, full of blackberry and black cherry flavors in juicy mouthfuls. The nose is complex, bold, and fun, with hints of black licorice, thyme, and pepper.

SPAIN

Older vines are common in Spain, producing concentrated berries with intense flavors.

MAJOR GRAPE VARIETIES: *White:*
Airén (mostly for budget whites); Albariño
(especially in Rías Baixas); Chardonnay,
Garnacha Blanca, Macabeo, Parellada, and
Xarel-lo (for Cava); Malvasia, Palomino,
Pedro Ximénez, and Moscatel (for Sherry);
Verdejo; Viura; *Red:* Cabernet Sauvignon,
Carignan (especially in Cariñena),
Garnacha, Merlot, Syrah, Tempranillo

MAJOR WINES PRODUCED: Cava;
Priorat; Rioja; Sherry; varietal, rosé, and
red blends from Cabernet Sauvignon,
Garnacha, Merlot, Monastrell, Syrah, and
Tempranillo; varietal whites from Albariño,
Chardonnay, and Verdejo

READING A SPANISH WINE LABEL

In addition to the information normally found on European wine labels (including regional designation), you might also encounter the following terms when shopping for Spanish wines:

Añejo: Old/aged

Barrica: Barrel

Bodega: A winery or cellar

Cosecha: Harvest

Denominación de Origen (DO): Wine sourced only from a designated region, with regulated growing, winemaking, and quality criteria

Denominación de Origen Calificada (DOCa): Highest quality wine, from a region with the strictest quality and control standards

Finca: Estate/farm (usually meaning the producer grows their own grapes)

Joven: Young (meant to be enjoyed upon release)

Roble: Oak

Rosado: Rosé

Semi-dulce: Medium-sweet style

Semi-seco: Off-dry style

Sin cosecha: Nonvintage

Vendimia: Vintage

Viñedo: Vineyard

Vino Blanco: White wine

Vino de la Tierra: Country wine

Vino de Mesa: Table wine

Vino Tinto: Red wine

The Iberian nation of Spain is the third-largest producer of wine by volume after Italy and France and, with almost three million acres of vineyards, takes the number-one spot for area under production. Grape cultivation in Spain stretches all the way back to around 3000 BCE. Spain's later colonization and missionary enterprises spread its grape varieties and winemaking knowledge far and wide in the "New World" (including establishing California's first vineyard and winery, in 1769).

Much of Spain's climate is hot and dry, with portions having a Mediterranean influence. Spain has little problem ripening grapes, which are often planted at higher elevations to mitigate the summer heat that the vines have to endure. Spain can do many wine styles well, and with nearly 140 wine regions, the country's wine scene is diverse and exciting.

A piece of classic wine geek trivia is that the Airén grape—used for brandy and budget white wines—is the most planted grape in Spain by area (especially in La Mancha, Spain's largest wine region, which produces about one-third of the country's wine). After Airén, red grapes rule, and Tempranillo is king: it's the backbone of Rioja's reds and rosés, and makes spicy, chewy-textured, medium- to full-bodied reds in Navarra, Ribera del Duero, and Rueda. Up-and-coming areas like Somontano are building reputations for producing wines from international varieties, including Cabernet Sauvignon.

Garnacha (Grenache) is widely planted throughout Spain, with older vines (some ranging from 50 to over 100 years old) not uncommon. Those older vines produce fewer, smaller berries, with higher skin-to-pulp ratios, and more concentrated, structured wines as a result. This is especially true in Priorat and Montsant, where Garnacha wines can be powerful, juicy, and deeply plummy (and pricey). The Navarra, Cariñena, Campo de Borja, and Calatayud regions all produce Garnacha, and many excellent bargain reds can be found there.

Here's a quick look at some of the most important wine styles made in Spain.

CAVA

"Cava" translates to "cellar"—a reference to where this Catalonia region's sparkling wines are stored to undergo secondary fermentation and age in bottles. So much Cava is made that the region was instrumental in the development of the gyropalette, a machine that automates the riddling process (see page 75) for sparkling wines. While you don't get the same grape varieties as Champagne (instead, the native Macabeo, Parellada, and Xarel-lo are used), you get the same production methods. Cavas don't match Champagnes in complexity or longevity, but they make up for it in delivering bang for the buck. Cava wines can have strong apple and toast aromas and flavors, a light body that feels creamy thanks to contact with yeasts, and a mousse that is both fun and refined. "Mousse" is used to describe the foam that forms when pouring a sparkling wine (and also refers to the airy sensation the foam and bubbles make in the mouth).

RIOJA

Situated along the Ebro River, Rioja is Spain's most famous wine region. Some white wines are made there (mostly from Viura grapes, in both tropically fruity and nutty, oxidative styles), as well as very good, wild strawberry–flavored rosés. But Rioja is best known for two things: red wines (based on Tempranillo) and oak aging. Rioja's quality tiers (Crianza, Reserva, and Gran Reserva) all have different aging requirements, with their time in wood dramatically impacting the amount of coconut, toast, cinnamon, and nut aromas and flavors in the wine (see the Tempranillo entry on page 56 for more details). While Rioja wines are already aged for you (they're ready to drink upon release), Reserva and Gran Reserva wines from excellent vintages can benefit from further bottle aging, developing earthy aromas and flavors.

SHERRY/JEREZ

Spain's unique fortified Sherry is produced near the Andalusian city of Jerez de la Frontera. It is not just "cooking wine"; in fact, good Sherry is one of the most unique wine drinking experiences, as its production relies on extensive oak aging. Sherry is fortified after completing fermentation, and uses an aging system called *solera* that blends older and younger wines together. Some Sherry styles age under a layer of yeasts called *flor*, which protects the wine from oxygen. The Palomino grape is used for most Sherries, because its base wine readily takes on the tertiary aromas and flavors from the aging process. (Pedro Ximénez or Moscatel grapes are used for sweeter styles.) The terms on a Sherry label are essential in understanding the production methods used, and the experience to expect in the glass.

Fino: Meaning "fine," these are dry, pale-amber Sherries, aged under *flor*, with aromas of almonds, and dried fig flavors.

Manzanilla: A lighter style of Fino specifically made near the port of Sanlúcar de Barrameda, resulting in salty aromas. There are also *Pasada* versions that are barrel-aged for longer periods, imparting nutty flavors and increasing their concentration.

Amontillado: Not just part of a great Edgar Allan Poe story, these are Fino sherries that are deliberately exposed to oxygen, making their aromas nuttier and their hue more amber.

Oloroso: Olorosos are usually dry and often reach alcohol levels up to 20 percent, from long barrel-aging that darkens and concentrates them, giving them greater richness in flavor and body. Sweeter styles are usually labeled as Cream Sherry.

Palo Cortado: This is basically an Amontillado that had its *flor* killed off, either accidentally or deliberately, exposing the wine to more oxygen in the barrels. They've got drier fruit flavors and a darker amber color.

Jerez Dulce: These are sweet sherries, often carrying "PX" on the label to designate the Pedro Ximénez grape. They are made from dried grapes, resulting in a color that is almost black. Intense and sweet, they offer roasted nut, chocolate, and rum aromas with dried fig and date flavors.

You can dive into wines from various Spanish regions in the following tastings:

- Cava in *Bubbles: From Budget to Big-Time* (page 76) and *Budget Wine Picks: Value at $10 and Under* (page 159)

- Ribera del Duero in *Wine + Food: Complement and Contrast* (page 176)

- Rioja in *The Tiers of Tempranillo in Rioja* (page 57)

- Sherry in *Fortified Wines: A Tasting Tutorial* (page 78)

Tempranillo vines thrive in Rioja, thanks to its warm growing season and diverse soil types.

UNITED STATES

Willamette Valley in Oregon has a temperate climate that is ideal for growing Pinot Noir.

MAJOR GRAPE VARIETIES: *White:* Chardonnay, Chenin Blanc, French Colombard, Gewürztraminer, Muscat of Alexandria, Muscat Blanc, Pinot Gris, Riesling, Sauvignon Blanc, Viognier; *Red:* Barbera, Cabernet Sauvignon, Cabernet Franc, Grenache, Merlot, Petite Sirah, Petit Verdot, Pinot Noir, Rubired and Ruby Cabernet, Syrah, Zinfandel

MAJOR WINES PRODUCED: Varietal and blended white, red, rosé, sparkling, and dessert (usually Late Harvest) wines; Bordeaux-style red blends (sometimes labeled "Meritage")

Attempts to make wine in North America date back to at least the 1500s, with varying levels of success. In what are now Florida, Virginia, and New Mexico, wine was crafted from both native varieties (which weren't to European settlers' tastes) and European varieties (which were killed by the phylloxera louse). By the 1800s, however, America enjoyed a booming wine industry, with grapes grown in states as diverse as Kentucky, California, and Ohio.

All of that changed in the early 20th century with Prohibition, which effectively outlawed any reasonable scale of wine production. The industry got clobbered and recovery was slow, with the best US wines rarely considered challengers to their European counterparts. A turning point came when California wines bested some of France's biggest names in the "Judgment of Paris" blind tasting competition of 1976, garnering worldwide attention. Winemakers in the United States never looked back, and now there are thousands of wineries here (including the top two producers by volume worldwide), with their best wines considered to be among the finest anywhere.

Wine in America is categorized into American Viticultural Areas (AVA), usually based on unique geographical and climatic combinations. This is very different from the European system, as it does not place requirements on winemaking techniques and grape varieties on AVAs. Grape varieties are usually listed on US wine labels, with the required percentage of how much of a stated variety must be used increasing as the AVA's size decreases.

CALIFORNIA

Nearly 90 percent of US wine production is concentrated on the West Coast, and that is dominated by one state: California. To give you some perspective, on its own California would be the fourth-largest wine producer *in the world*.

Spanish missionaries first brought European vines to what is now California hundreds of years ago, but the state's modern wine business really got started after Prohibition's repeal. In the 1960s, now iconic producers such as Heitz Wine Cellars and Robert Mondavi Winery were founded. The quality-first culture engendered by those pioneers has not let up in the ensuing half century.

California is huge, so let's consider it in terms of its four primary regions.

North Coast

The North Coast covers about three million acres over six counties, all of them north of San Francisco, and includes the most famous AVAs in the United States: Napa Valley and Sonoma County. The common thread is the influence of the Pacific Ocean, which is channeled inland via cooling breezes and fog,

READING AN AMERICAN WINE LABEL

Wine labels from the United States are among the easiest to read, as they usually include the grape variety and the region where they were harvested (see the label example below). Here is some other information you might find:

Bottled by: Winery bottled the wine, which may have been fermented and aged elsewhere

Contains sulfites: Mandatory warning for any wine that uses sulfites

Estate bottled: Winery grew the grapes and produced and bottled the wine on its property

Made and bottled by: Bottler fermented at least 75 percent of the wine

Produced and bottled by: Bottler fermented 75 percent or more of the wine at the label's stated address

Reserve: Unregulated marketing term, usually referring to an oak-aged wine

Vintage: Designation indicating the year the grapes were harvested

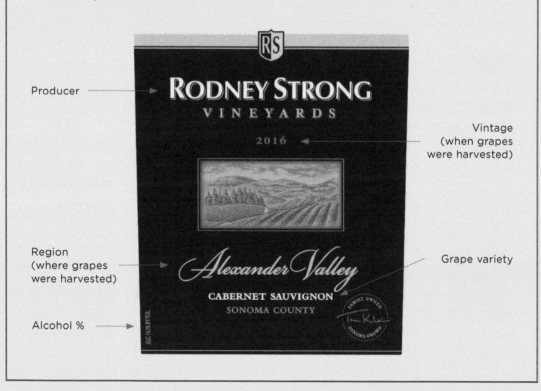

Producer

RODNEY STRONG
VINEYARDS

2016

Vintage (when grapes were harvested)

Region (where grapes were harvested)

Alexander Valley

CABERNET SAUVIGNON
SONOMA COUNTY

Grape variety

Alcohol %

helping offset the area's dry, hot conditions. This effect is essential for growing the ripe but balanced grapes that go into the region's wines.

Despite making only a tiny percentage of California's wine production, Napa Valley and its sub-AVAs (including Howell Mountain, Mount Veeder, Oakville, Rutherford, Stags' Leap, and Yountville) see a disproportionate amount of attention, because its best wines can compete against the world's greatest. Cabernet Sauvignon and Chardonnay are king and queen, making full-bodied, lush, age-worthy wines that have dense fruit flavors and rich aromatics. Merlot, Sauvignon Blanc, and their related Bordeaux-style blended wines are also important. They're big wines, often carrying large price tags to match.

The much larger Sonoma County is nearly as famous as its neighbor. This is one of the most diverse wine regions in the United States, and includes Alexander Valley, Chalk Hill, Dry Creek Valley, Knights Valley, Los Carneros, Russian River Valley, and Sonoma Coast, among others. Like Napa, much Chardonnay and Cabernet Sauvignon are made, often slightly higher in acidity and herbal aromas while retaining a similar sense of ripeness. Pinot Noir is a standout, with cooler coastal regions making expressive reds that are full and fresh in the mouth. Zinfandel has long had a foothold here, where it achieves balance on the palate and spicy complexity on the nose, and is beloved for its jammy fruit flavors.

Another notable AVA in the North Coast is Mendocino, which includes Anderson Valley AVA. Cabernet Sauvignon and Chardonnay dominate, but

Sonoma's Alexander Valley has an ideal climate for growing several grape varieties.

its full-bodied Pinot Noirs are also impressive. Its varied microclimates create pockets of diversity where many grapes can grow, including Gewürztraminer, Riesling, Chenin Blanc, Grenache, Merlot, and Petit Verdot, and the area is a pioneer in organic and sustainable grape farming. Across the Mayacamas Mountains from Mendocino sits Lake County, which sees cooling effects from its proximity to Clear Lake. Lake County grows a few dozen grape varieties, but its most prominent wines are made from Cabernet Sauvignon and Merlot.

Central Coast

This large region covers the area from San Francisco Bay down to Santa Barbara County. A lot of wine is made here; over 50,000 acres are planted to Chardonnay. Many AVAs here specialize in balanced, expressive Chardonnays and highly aromatic, juicy Pinot Noirs, particularly Monterey County, Sta. Rita Hills, Santa Barbara County, and San Luis Obispo. Edna Valley is one of the region's most diverse AVAs, offering Sauvignon Blanc, Viognier, and Syrah wines that often over-deliver for their prices. Paso Robles is also found here, a unique region that does Cabernet Sauvignon especially well, with fully ripened tannins that give the wines bold but smooth palates. One of California's most historic AVAs, Livermore Valley, is part of the Central Coast. Much of the Cabernet Sauvignon and Chardonnay planted throughout California can be traced back to vine clones first cultivated there, which still produces some of the best deals going for both varieties in the state.

Central Valley

This region, near the Sierra Nevada Mountains, has the California Gold Rush to thank for introducing grape vines to the area. It includes the Sierra Foothills and Lodi AVAs, both of which are famous for concentrated, jammy, spicy Zinfandel, some of it from vines that are among California's oldest. They are great wine regions to explore for bargain hunters who love full-bodied reds.

South Coast

This is where viticulture in California began, with vines planted by missionaries, and it covers a large area: from Ventura County through Los Angeles and San Diego, all the way to the Mexican border in the south. Most of the region shares latitude with Northern Africa, and so is hot and dry. But cooling influences from the Pacific Ocean help offset the heat, allowing good ripening conditions for full-bodied Grenache, Cabernet Sauvignon, and Zinfandel. The Temecula Valley AVA is located here, as is Ventura County, both of which are seeing exciting wine developments by small, passionate producers.

California Dreaming: Benchmark Wines from Cali

It's impossible to cover all of California in one tasting, but thankfully there are some iconic brands that can provide an introduction to what has made wine-making there so successful. This tasting takes a look at a few of those wines.

Au Bon Climat Chardonnay (Santa Barbara County, Central Coast)

Winemaker Jim Clendenen brought his perfectionist streak to crafting wines near Santa Barbara, resulting in this classic, gold-hued, medium-bodied Chardonnay. There are aromas of smoke, spice, vanilla, and lemons, flavors of peaches and brioche, and a nice line of acidity that makes this a white worth aging.

Robert Mondavi Winery Fumé Blanc (Napa Valley, North Coast)

The winery that put Napa Valley on the global wine map also created a signature style, namely this oak-aged Sauvignon Blanc/Sémillon blend. Full-bodied and crafted much like Bordeaux's best whites, this wine has light-gold hues. Lemon curd, herbs, flint, and white flowers mark the nose, while opulent tropical fruits and richness grace the palate.

Rodney Strong Vineyards Pinot Noir (Russian River Valley, North Coast)

Russian River Valley can offer Pinots that are at once delicate and powerful, as in this fuller-bodied, garnet-colored sipper from Sonoma's Rodney Strong. Orange peel, cranberry, and oak spice notes abound, with rich, juicy cherry fruitiness in the mouth.

Eberle Vineyard Select Cabernet Sauvignon (Paso Robles, Central Coast)

Former college football star Gary Eberle nearly created the Paso Robles Cabernet market on his own, and his Vineyard Select red is still a benchmark for the region. Opaque garnet in the glass, plum, cedar, and graphite notes greet your nose, while the palate is dense and structured with delicious cassis flavors and tannins that feel silky rather than harsh.

Ravenswood Old Vine Zinfandel (Lodi, Central Valley)

Ravenswood founder Joel Peterson is regarded as the godfather of California Zin, and we wouldn't have today's robust red Zinfandel market without him. Speaking of robust, it's a perfect descriptor for this purple, spicy, hedonistic, full-bodied wine. It has blueberry, vanilla, and plum aromas, and lush, ripe blackberry flavors that feel juicy and inviting.

OREGON

Most of Oregon was once thought too cold for growing wine grapes. That assumption was shattered in the late 1970s, when the Eyrie Vineyards' Oregon Pinot Noir began winning awards and wowing critics. Today, Oregon's Willamette Valley is famous for small-production, excellent Pinot Noirs that combine delicate aromatics with complex berry fruit flavors, and a fresh but structured palate. Pinot Gris is made into fleshy, fruity white wines throughout Oregon, and Chardonnay is increasingly being recognized as one of the state's premium grapes.

Southern Oregon is dry and warm, with some spots sharing more climate similarities to inland California than northern Oregon. There, different varieties are showing promise, such as Cabernet Sauvignon, Grenache, Merlot, and Malbec.

WASHINGTON STATE

Washington is the United States' second-largest wine producer and one of its most exciting. It produces wines from a diverse set of grape varieties, including Chardonnay, Riesling, Gewürztraminer, Cabernet Sauvignon, Merlot, Syrah (which is exceptional in its higher-end wines), Grenache, and Petit Verdot. The state's diversity comes from two important factors: unique geology and soils created by Ice Age flooding and a warm, dry climate east of the Cascade Mountains, where most of its grapes are grown.

The majority of Washington wine comes from Columbia Valley, its largest AVA (and one that it shares with Oregon), covering nearly a quarter of the state. In this area, the sun shines about 300 days per year, making it easy to produce ripe, medium-bodied white wines, as well as full-bodied red wines with smooth, silky tannins. Cabernet Sauvignon in particular benefits from Eastern Washington's weather, making wines with good structure that are delicious while young. (Not surprisingly, Washington is renowned for its high quality, affordable Bordeaux-style red blends.) Western Washington has become a stateside tourist mecca for wine geeks, with a high concentration of tasting rooms and wine-themed events in the town of Woodinville.

NEW YORK

New York State has four distinct wine regions: Lake Erie, Hudson River Region, Long Island, and the Finger Lakes, with the latter two garnering the most media attention. While New York's climate is thoroughly continental (with cold winters and hot summers), cold climate grape varieties can fare well there when planted near bodies of water (which help mitigate the chill). For Long Island, this helping hand is provided by the Atlantic Ocean, Long Island Sound, and Peconic Bay. In the Finger Lakes, vines are planted near several deep, narrow glacial lakes, which help regulate the temperatures in the vineyards.

Hardy, hybrid American grape varieties are widely planted in New York, as they can withstand the cold winters. But the best of the state's wines are crafted using European varieties. For Long Island, these include Merlot, Cabernet Franc, and Chardonnay, all of which are leaner and lighter than those from California. The Finger Lakes specializes in light- to medium-bodied Riesling (dry, off-dry, and sweet), the best reaching world-class status, especially those from Seneca Lake (Gewürztraminer and Pinot Noir also excel in warmer vintages).

Long Island is one of New York's most vibrant wine regions.

OTHER AMERICAN WINE REGIONS

Wine is made in some form or another in every single US state. Here are a few of the most exciting wine developments happening across the continental United States.

Mid-Atlantic Seaboard: The Mid-Atlantic shares latitude with some of the most famous wine regions in Western Europe and has similar ocean influences. So it's no surprise that states like Maryland, New Jersey, and Pennsylvania have seen a growth in small producers crafting lighter, earthier wine styles from European grapes like Cabernet Sauvignon and Merlot, as well as French-American hybrids like Chambourcin.

Virginia: Virginia is fast becoming one of the most promising wine-growing states, specializing in higher-acid Viognier and Petit Manseng whites and burly reds made from the native Norton grape.

Michigan: This state is able to grow grapes near the Great Lakes, which help mitigate the region's cold climate. Riesling does particularly well here.

Texas: While warm, Texas enjoys several microclimates (especially in the Hill Country and High Plains areas) that favor bold red wines made from Cabernet Sauvignon and Tempranillo.

Arizona/New Mexico: The southeastern portion of Arizona has seen a wine-producing explosion, with the state now hosting over 100 wineries, and growing several varieties (with the most intriguing reds being made from Sangiovese, Mourvèdre, and Cabernet Franc, and whites from Malvasia). Neighboring New Mexico has been growing grapes for nearly 400 years and now makes wines from many varieties, including Cabernet Sauvignon, Zinfandel, Sangiovese, Gewürztraminer, Chardonnay, and Chenin Blanc.

Colorado: The lofty elevations of Colorado (including some of the highest vine plantings in the world) allow wine grapes to get plenty of sunlight while retaining their acidity. Colorado's wine scene is vibrant and diverse; Merlot, Cabernet Sauvignon, Syrah, and Cabernet Franc do well there for reds, while Chardonnay, Riesling, and Viognier are the standout whites.

Idaho: Given its proximity to the grape-growing areas of Washington and Oregon, it was only a matter of time before Idaho got in on the modern US wine scene. Riesling and Syrah are standouts from the state, with Malbec, Merlot, and Petite Sirah also showing promise.

Born in the USA: America's Wine Regions

There's more to US wine than California, folks. Here are some excellent examples of wines made in various states, from sea to shining sea.

Fox Run Vineyards Dry Riesling (Finger Lakes, New York)
Pale-gold, with intense lime aromas and a light palate, this exudes a sense of purity in its lemon-lime and fresh pear flavors. Its high acidity makes the texture feel almost jaunty in the mouth, while its emphasis on fruitiness signals that it's decidedly "New World" (even if it's inspired stylistically by its European counterparts).

Barboursville Vineyards Reserve Viognier (Virginia)
White is the name of the game with this Virginian Viognier—as in a white wine with white peach flavors, white flower aromas, and notes of white pepper. There are flavors of lemon, too, and a medium-bodied palate that feels juicy while still being lively.

Wolffer Estate 'Classic Red' (Long Island, New York)
This red wine is aptly named, as it recreates the classic Bordeaux-style blend (utilizing Malbec, Merlot, Cabernet Sauvignon, Cabernet Franc, and Petit Verdot, depending on the vintage) with a New York twist. European in style with an acid-driven, savory palate, there are flavors of cassis and red plums, with spice notes like toast, licorice, chocolate, and cedar (from its time in oak).

Elk Cove Vineyards Estate Pinot Noir (Willamette Valley, Oregon)
While Oregon Pinot Noir can get expensive, Elk Cove manages to create an ambassador red for the region without charging an arm and a leg. Ruby-red and full of Oregon Pinot's distinctive cherry and black tea leaf aromas, it's medium-bodied, with fleshy fruit flavors of red plum and red currants.

Pedernales Cellars Texas Tempranillo (Texas High Plains, Texas)
Spain's signature grape feels right at home in Texas. With tobacco spice, leather, clove, and black cherry on the nose and plummy fruit flavors on a medium-bodied palate, this is a crowd-pleasing red that is a natural match for Texas barbecue.

ARGENTINA

Vine plantings can reach the edges of the Andes in Argentina.

MAJOR GRAPE VARIETIES: *White:* Chardonnay, Muscat of Alexandria, Sauvignon Blanc, Torrontés; *Red:* Bonarda, Cabernet Sauvignon, Malbec, Pinot Noir, Syrah, Tempranillo

MAJOR WINES PRODUCED: Varietal Bonarda, Malbec, Pinot Noir, Torrontés

Argentina is now the fifth-largest wine producer worldwide, a stunning achievement for a country that didn't start seriously exporting its wines until the 1990s. That focus on exports created a quality revolution in Argentine winemaking, much to the benefit of wine lovers around the globe. With its abundant sunlight and lack of rain, the trick in Argentina is utilizing elevation and irrigation (with water from the Andes) to keep the grapes from getting *too* ripe.

Argentina's wine production is often credited to European immigrants who, fleeing the phylloxera epidemic in Europe in the 19th century, brought grape varieties and winemaking experience with them. But Argentina's winemaking history actually stretches back to the 1500s, when vines were planted by Spanish colonizers and missionaries. The most important development for Argentine wine, however, might have come in the 1850s, when President Domingo Faustino Sarmiento requested grapevine cuttings from France. Among those cuttings was Malbec, which would become the country's signature grape. (This event is now celebrated every April 17 as "World Malbec Day," which is a great idea for a themed tasting!)

France's Malbec took especially well to the country's semi-arid, high desert climate, in which the phylloxera louse never managed to spread widely. Here, Malbec takes on a ripe, plummy depth that it seldom achieves in its home country.

MENDOZA

Mendoza is Argentina's most important wine region, responsible for two-thirds of the country's output. Vineyard plantings in Mendoza reach over 2,000 feet above sea level on average, which allows for cooling effects on the grapes at night (helping preserve acidity), while providing ample sunlight for ripening during the day (to develop mature flavors and tannins). Harvests here are dry and warm, with soils that have very low fertility, making for some of the most ideal grape growing conditions to be found anywhere on Earth. Mendoza is also historically important for Argentine winemaking, with the Jesuits having planted grapevines here in the mid-1500s (using viticulture practices established earlier by the region's indigenous peoples).

With relatively low costs for land and labor, wines from Mendoza can be incredible bargains, particularly for juicy, plummy, full-bodied Malbec reds and floral, tropical, and round Torrontés whites. More premium wines (from the Luján de Cuyo and Uco Valley areas) are being produced from vineyards in the foothills of the Andes, some planted up to 5,000 feet above sea level.

SALTA

In the northwest, Salta, and its subregion Cafayate in particular, have a more moderate climate (thanks to its high altitude, which mitigates the effects of the region's low latitude) and produce somewhat more herbal expressions of Malbec that are still bold, ripe, and powerful. With the highest vineyards planted at a dizzying 9,000 feet above sea level, the vines experience large temperature changes from day to night (in some cases, swinging between 100°F and 50°F), preserving acidity and aromatics in the grapes. The mountainous terrain in Salta also creates a rain barrier, shielding the vineyards from precipitation and allowing ample sunlight hours to ripen grapes. When needed, snowmelt from the mountains also provides plenty of water for irrigation.

PATAGONIA

Patagonia is a unique outlier for Argentina. This area of rugged terrain, dinosaur fossils, glaciers, and penguins is also home to some of the most southerly vineyards in the world. The desert-like territory here is large, covering an area nearly twice the size of the state of California, with viticulture possible only in proximity to rivers (created from water provided by the nearby Andes mountains). The altitude of vineyards here is relatively low by Argentine standards, though still an impressive 1,000 feet above sea level. Patagonia's very cool nights favor grape varieties like Pinot Noir.

Mountainous terrain shields the vineyards of Argentina's Salta region from rain, providing ample sunlight to ripen grapes.

Argentina: Sunny Side Up

Argentina sees some of the highest levels of sunshine of any wine country, which makes ripening grapes to their full potential a breeze for its growers. This tasting introduces us to many of Argentina's most asado-friendly varieties (so fire up the grill!).

Colomé Torrontés (Salta)

Aromas of melon, jasmine, and blossoms burst from this yellow-tinged, aromatic white. Salta's unique climate and high elevation help the aromatic lift of the wine, while its ample sunlight allows the grapes to express their ripe fruit flavors and strong body. Medium-bodied and broad in the mouth, tropical fruit and grape flavors make this sipper a nice match for appetizers.

Bodega Aniello Riverside Estate '006' Pinot Noir (Patagonia)

From the southernmost (and coolest) of Argentina's wine regions comes this pale ruby, medium-bodied Pinot, a variety that has great potential here but would struggle in warmer Mendoza. Rose, cranberry, and wood spice aromas kick things off, with wild strawberry flavors dancing on a textured palate that is refreshing and structured.

Argento Bonarda (Mendoza)

Opaque red and medium-bodied, this wine is deliciously gulpable, full of raspberries and plum aromas. The palate is awash in vanilla, blackberry, and red grape flavors, all packaged in a silky-feeling mouthful. Its approachable, juicy texture is a direct result of how well Bonarda (originally from Italy) ripens in Mendoza.

Zuccardi 'Serie A' Malbec (Mendoza)

Deep shades of reddish purple greet your eyes with this spicy red wine. Full-bodied and velvety, it starts with tobacco, vanilla, prune, and dark berry aromas and ends with ripe, wild, black and blue fruit flavors. It's a wine with deep fruit flavors that's a great example of Argentina's ability to produce bold, complex versions of Malbec at good prices.

CHILE

Viticulture in Chile's Casablanca Valley is possible thanks to the cooling influence of the Pacific Ocean.

MAJOR GRAPE VARIETIES: *White:* Chardonnay, Muscatel, Sauvignon Blanc; *Red:* Cabernet Franc, Cabernet Sauvignon, Carignan, Carménère, Malbec, Merlot, País, Pinot Noir, Syrah

MAJOR WINES PRODUCED: Bordeaux-style red blends, varietal Cabernet Sauvignon, Carignan (especially premium reds), Carménère, Chardonnay (especially budget wines), Merlot, Sauvignon Blanc

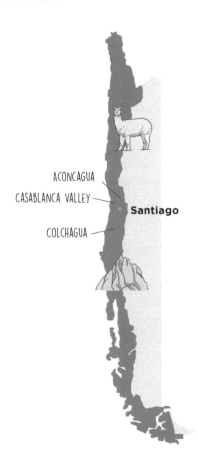

ACONCAGUA

CASABLANCA VALLEY — • **Santiago**

COLCHAGUA

Missionaries and conquistadors from Spain likely first brought vines to Chile during the 1550s. As a colony, Chile's wine industry was hamstrung by Spain for centuries, mostly producing sweet País and Muscatel wines. The 18th century changed everything, when wealthy Chileans began importing vines from France in an attempt to replicate the red wine magic of Bordeaux. They succeeded, and now Chile specializes in Bordeaux grapes, as well as growing some portion of nearly every major European wine grape variety but using wine labeling laws similar to those in the United States.

Given Chile's narrow (just over 200 miles) and long (about 2,600 miles) geography, you might expect temperatures would cool as you move from north to south, and you'd be right. But Chile's global position is unique: it is surrounded by natural borders, with the Andes to the east, the Atlantic Ocean to the west, Antarctica to the south, and the Atacama Desert to the north. Not only does this protect Chile from many natural pests (allowing farmers to avoid the added expense of grafting their grapevines), it also creates vineyard microclimates, with cool air from the Atlantic's Humboldt Current channeling into many of Chile's vineyards. The cooling influence moderates Chile's Mediterranean climates, allowing grapes to ripen well while maintaining fresh acidity and powerful (typically herbal) aromatics. These are leaner, more focused wines than are found in Argentina, Chile's eastern neighbor.

Most of Chile's wine regions are concentrated toward the center of the country. While the Aconcagua region is important for premium Bordeaux-style red blends (along with noteworthy whites from Casablanca Valley) Chile's most important region by far is the Central Valley, where the vast majority of its wines are made. This region includes the Curicó, Maipo, Maule, and Rapel valleys, and the well-regarded subregions of Colchagua and Casablanca Valley.

Bordeaux's major red and white varieties are planted throughout the region, but Central Valley is most associated with Carménère. This long-neglected red blending grape was planted widely, having been mistaken for Merlot (which grows similarly shaped leaves). Carménère has become a flagship variety here, adding structural backbone, color, and herbal spice aromatics to red blends. It has done so well that Chile now grows over 90 percent of all Carménère worldwide. Many varietal Carménère wines from Central Valley can be found, which offer deep black cherry fruit flavors, tobacco and herbal spice notes, and deliciously full-bodied palates.

Chile: Land of Diversity

Chile's long and thin geography means that it has varied microclimates, with unique combinations of temperature differences (north to south), and ocean influences (west to east). This tasting will show you how those differences play out in Chile's diverse wine scene.

Emiliana 'Natura' Sauvignon Blanc (Casablanca Valley)

Within this area, cooled by the Atlantic Ocean's Humboldt Current, Sauvignon Blanc thrives in Emiliana's organic vineyards. Light yellow in hue, herbal aromatic complexity combines with grapefruit flavors and lemongrass notes to deliver a lighter-bodied, vibrant white.

De Martino Legado Reserva Chardonnay (Limarí Valley)

Limarí sees little rainfall, sitting at about the same point as Egypt and Iraq do in the Northern Hemisphere. Thanks to the coastal "Camanchaca" fog, however, a cooling influence is provided that, combined with the area's limestone soils, favors white wine production. This pale gold Chardonnay has aromas of apricots, ripe white peaches, and nuts, and a gorgeous, full-bodied palate that tastes of stone fruits, with a hint of saline.

Leyda Pinot Noir (Leyda Valley)

Ledya Valley has direct access to cooling Atlantic Ocean breezes, making its vineyards an ideal home for lighter reds like Pinot Noir. This incarnation, from the producer that takes the valley's name, only sees mild oak treatment. The result is a transparent ruby color, a nose of raspberries and herbs, and a pure, medium-bodied palate full of juicy cherry fruit flavors.

Casa Silva 'Colección' Carménère (Colchagua)

The consistently warm Colchagua allows red grapes to enjoy a long, slow ripening curve. Casa Silva takes advantage of this terroir in their Carménère, which is unashamedly full-bodied. An inky purple in the glass, dark fruit, tobacco, and green herb aromas are followed by a black cherry–flavored palate that's round and intense.

AUSTRALIA

Australia is the source of some of the world's best Shiraz and Riesling wines.

MAJOR GRAPE VARIETIES: *White:* Chardonnay, Riesling, Sauvignon Blanc, Sémillon; *Red:* Cabernet Sauvignon, Grenache, Merlot, Mourvèdre, Muscat à Petits Grains Rouge, Pinot Noir, Shiraz

MAJOR WINES PRODUCED: Varietal wines from Cabernet Sauvignon, Chardonnay, Merlot, Pinot Noir, Riesling, and Shiraz; Syrah/Grenache/Mourvèdre red blends; Sauvignon Blanc/Sémillon blended whites; sparkling wine (mainly in Tasmania); fortified dessert wines (Rutherglen Muscat)

Australia's first ill-fated attempt at winemaking started in the 1700s with vine cuttings brought to the penal colony of New South Wales, where the heat and humidity rotted the vines. But by the 1800s, Australia was officially exporting wine, and it hasn't slowed down since (today it exports 780 million liters per year). Australia's best winemaking regions are mostly concentrated near the southeast coast and have warm, dry, Mediterranean climates. Local talent, combined with expertise over the years from "flying winemakers" (who spent off-seasons from the Northern Hemisphere making wine in the Southern Hemisphere, and vice versa) has established the country as one of the world's leading producers of several European grapes, including Shiraz (Syrah), Riesling, and Cabernet Sauvignon.

Australia is divided into five main wine regions:

Western Australia: This region includes Margaret River on the far southwest coast, where sea influences moderate the climate, allowing for the development of rich, complex Chardonnay whites and expressive, aromatic Cabernet Sauvignon reds.

South Australia: Located in the central south, this region contains several famous winemaking areas, such as Barossa Valley and McLaren Vale (both known for spicy, powerfully full-bodied, silky Shiraz reds), Clare and Eden valleys (which produce dry, steely, and fruit-forward Rieslings), and Coonawarra (known for Shiraz, and also expressive, structured Cabernet Sauvignons grown on its red clay "terra rossa" soils).

New South Wales: Situated near the far southeastern shores, New South Wales includes Hunter Valley, famous for textural, complex, and age-worthy Sémillon whites.

Victoria: Located just south of New South Wales, this region includes Beechworth (notable for spicy, refined Pinot Noirs), Yarra Valley (where lithe, mineral, and acid-driven Chardonnay is made), and Rutherglen (whose dessert wine—Rutherglen Muscat—is reminiscent of Madeira and uses similar production techniques).

Tasmania: This large island to Australia's south enjoys a cooler climate and is having success with lovely, traditional-method sparkling wines.

Australia and New Zealand: Deliciousness from "Down Undah"

There are a few wine styles that have become iconic from the "Down Undah" and "Kiwi" nations. This tasting takes a look at what has made them both famous.

Kim Crawford Sauvignon Blanc (Marlborough, New Zealand)

The most iconic variety from what might be New Zealand's most iconic producer, this pale-yellow wine nearly explodes with citrus, exotic fruits, and herbs on the nose. The palate is medium-bodied, with fleshiness to balance the acidity coming from all of those lemon and grapefruit flavors. Through it all, this wine showcases the boldly aromatic style that has become the identity of New Zealand Sauvignon Blanc.

Innocent Bystander Pinot Noir (Central Otago, New Zealand)

Light ruby in color and medium weight in the mouth, wood spice (from oak aging), lavender, tea, and cherry aromas are followed by juicy flavors of red berry compote, and Pinot's signature lively acidity.

Tyrrell's Sémillon (Hunter Valley, Australia)

This Bordeaux white grape shines in Hunter Valley. Yellow in the glass, light-bodied in the mouth, and bursting with lemon-like acidity, there are aromas of white flowers, grapefruit, pears, and herbal spices. The palate has focus, with apple flavors and Sémillon's intriguing, piquant texture.

Peter Lehmann Portrait Shiraz (Barossa, Australia)

Medium in body and big on value, this deep ruby-red is quintessential Barossa Shiraz, an area that produces ripe grapes that retain their spice notes. Pepper and bramble aromas, along with chocolate and vanilla, give way to a silky palate full of rich black raspberry fruitiness.

Chambers Rosewood Rutherglen Muscat (Rutherglen, Australia)

Made from aged Muscat à Petit Grains grapes, this is almost copper-colored in the glass from long periods spent in large, old oak barrels, where the wine slowly interacts with oxygen and becomes more concentrated. It's an affordable example of Australia's answer to Madeira and is full of cinnamon, orange rind, and cedar aromas, with hints of dried white figs and sultana. Rich and full, its dried fruit flavors are sweet without feeling cloying.

NEW ZEALAND

A beautiful setting for beautiful wines: South Island, New Zealand

MAJOR GRAPE VARIETIES: *White:* Chardonnay, Pinot Gris, Riesling, Sauvignon Blanc; *Red:* Merlot, Pinot Noir, Syrah

MAJOR WINES PRODUCED: Varietal Pinot Noir, Sauvignon Blanc, Syrah

NORTH ISLAND

HAWKE'S BAY

Wellington

MARLBOROUGH

SOUTH ISLAND

The South Pacific islands of New Zealand have a vinous history that dates back to its colonial era, when wine was made there for British troops in the 1800s. It took some time for the wine business to grow, but by the 1980s New Zealand Sauvignon Blanc was winning international acclaim, and the country's wine expansion was officially on; it now exports a whopping 90 percent of its production.

NORTH ISLAND

New Zealand enjoys a maritime climate that varies from north to south, and its wine regions are generally divided into its two main islands. The North Island is home to Hawke's Bay, the oldest (and second-largest) of New Zealand's wine regions. Gimblett Gravels, noted for its cooler-climate, peppery, lighter-bodied Syrah reds, can be found there. Also located there is Martinborough, another cooler-climate area that is producing elegant, fresh, high-end Pinot Noir.

SOUTH ISLAND

The South Island includes Marlborough, where the largest volume of NZ wine is made and where 70 percent of its vineyard area is located. Sauvignon Blanc dominates here, where it creates fruity, abundantly aromatic whites, ranging in styles from slightly off-dry and full to clean and racy. South Island's other major wine region is Central Otago, which has the country's highest elevation vineyards in a continental microclimate that produces structured, medium-bodied Pinot Noir.

GERMANY

Difficult farming is a hallmark of the steep, picturesque vineyards of the Mosel in Germany.

MAJOR GRAPE VARIETIES: *White:* Grauburgunder (Pinot Gris), Müller-Thurgau (Rivaner), Riesling, Silvaner, Weißburgunder (Pinot Blanc); *Red:* Dornfelder, Spätburgunder (Pinot Noir)

MAJOR WINES PRODUCED: Varietal whites from Gewürztraminer, Grauburgunder; Müller-Thurgau, Riesling, Silvaner, and Weißburgunder; varietal reds from Dornfelder and Spätburgunder; Eiswein (Icewine); Sekt (sparkling wine)

READING A GERMAN WINE LABEL

German wine labels are tricky to read. That's partly due to the use of grape ripeness category terms for their highest quality tier wines (Qualitätswein mit Prädikat), which makes sense when you consider that getting wine grapes to fully ripen in Germany's cold climate can be challenging. Here are terms that you're likely to see:

Kabinett: Using the least ripe grapes; somewhat sweet and low in alcohol

Spätlese: Made with ripe grapes, in both dry and slightly sweet styles

Auslese: Made from select bunches of grapes left on the vine until they reach higher sugar levels and, sometimes, a touch of botrytis (see page 24); usually sweet and often ages well in the bottle

Beerenauslese: Using grapes selected berry by berry, and infected with botrytis; always sweet and meant for dessert

Trockenbeerenauslese: Using only selected berries that are raisined and heavily infected with botrytis; these are complex, syrupy wines with incredibly high residual sugar levels

Additionally, you might also see these terms:

Deutscher Tafelwein: Table wine

Deutscher Landwein: Country wine

Qualitätswein bestimmter Anbaugebiete (QbA): "Quality wine from designated cultivation areas," wine sourced only from a designated region, with regulated growing, winemaking, and quality criteria

Qualitätswein mit Prädikat (QmP): Highest quality wine, from a region with the strictest standards (usually with ripeness designation)

Trocken: "Dry"

Halbtrocken: "Half-dry"

Feinherb: "Off-dry" (the term is not officially regulated)

Eiswein: Made from grapes that freeze on the vine, concentrating their sugars and intensity to about the same level as Beerenauslese

Germany grows over 130 grape varieties, most of them for white wine. Why? Because this European nation has some of the most northerly vineyards on the globe, and its cold, continental climate demands grape varieties that can withstand a long, slow ripening curve. Historically, Germany is rich in wine tradition, with Charlemagne having planted vines along the Rhine river and Riesling being referenced in documents as far back as the 1400s (and Pinot Noir as far back as the 1300s).

Germany's wine labeling laws are notoriously complicated puzzles for those of us who don't know German (for a primer on how to read them, see page 145). They are puzzles worth solving, however, because Germany is the de facto standard for Riesling worldwide. Simply put, no other country fully expresses the scope of Riesling's aromatics and flavors from citrus to apples to quince to apricots to you-name-it. These are the most important spots to know.

Baden: Germany's southernmost, sunniest, and warmest (by German standards) region, known for its lighter-bodied, structured, and aromatic Pinot Noir reds.

Mosel: One of the world's benchmark regions for Riesling, which is grown mostly on slate soils on the steep banks of the Mosel river. The Riesling style here favors off-dry, lighter-bodied whites with crisp acidity, floral aromas, and pronounced minerality.

Nahe: Soils near the river Nahe vary in content, allowing the region to offer differing expressions of grapes such as Müller-Thurgau and Riesling.

Pfalz: One of the larger wine regions in Germany, with a climate similar to its neighbors Alsace and Baden. The area is seeing an increase in red wine production, mostly the velvety, plummy, fresh reds from the Dornfelder grape. Riesling still dominates here, however, primarily in drier versions with increased body and power.

Rheingau: A small but historic region along the bend of the Rhine river and the birthplace of much of Germany's winemaking style. Balance is the hallmark of Rheingau's drier Rieslings, which are powerful, aromatic, and feel steely but also accessible.

Rheinhessen: Germany's largest wine region and one of its most important, the Rheinhessen is the home of the infamous "Liebfraumilch" wines made from Müller-Thurgau. Dry and sweet reds (primarily from Dornfelder) are made, but Riesling is the rising star, made in just about every style, with medium-bodied, drier versions becoming increasingly popular.

Germany: Northern Delights

Exploring German wine means exploring Riesling above all else. But as you'll see in this tasting, Riesling isn't the only delightful grape that takes well to Germany's northern climes.

Dönnhoff Estate Riesling (Nahe)
The Nahe is notable for its volcanic vineyard soils, which produce distinctively flavored Riesling grapes. This pale-yellow Riesling is approachable and fun, with a vibrant, light body, aromas of white flowers and limes, and crisp apple flavors in the mouth, with a hint of sweetness.

Dr. Pauly-Bergweiler Noble House Riesling (Mosel)
This lighter-bodied, light-gold Riesling is a good ambassador for the Mosel's lovely, floral whites, with aromas of peaches, lime zest, and honeysuckle. On the palate, lemon and white peach flavors are combined with a light sweetness, balanced by energetic freshness.

Weingut Markgraf Von Baden Spätburgunder Bermatinger (Baden)
Germany makes more dry (trocken) Pinot Noir (Spätburgunder) than you might imagine, though much of it tends to stay within the country's borders. From Germany's southern, and somewhat warmer, Baden region comes this Pinot Noir red. Ruby in the glass, this lighter-bodied Pinot shows notes of earth, herbs, and raspberries with flavors of tart cranberry and red plums.

P. J. Valckenberg Dornfelder (Rheinhessen)
This Dornfelder (a red variety that originated in Germany) is medium-bodied and dark red in the glass, opening with cherry and wild herb aromas and offering flavors of ripe blackberry, vanilla, and a hint of sweetness.

Fitz-Ritter Gewürztraminer Spätlese (Pfalz)
In the Pfalz, a bit of warmth and ample amounts of sunlight allow several varieties to thrive, including Gewürztraminer. Here, Fitz-Ritter offers a ripe (Spätlese) version of that grape, which is amber-yellow, juicy, and medium-bodied. You'll find notes of flowers, spices, and peaches, along with flavors of tangerine and a touch of candied lemon peel.

PORTUGAL

Few wine regions match the visual drama of the Douro in Portugal.

MAJOR GRAPE VARIETIES: *White:*
Alvarinho, Antão Vaz, Arinto, Encruzado,
Loureiro, Malvasia, Verdelho; *Red:* Alicante
Bouschet, Castelão, Tempranillo (aka Tinta
Roriz or Aragonez), Touriga Franca, Touriga
Nacional, Trincadeira

MAJOR WINES PRODUCED: Alentejo
red and white blends, Douro red blends,
Madeira, Port, Vinho Verde

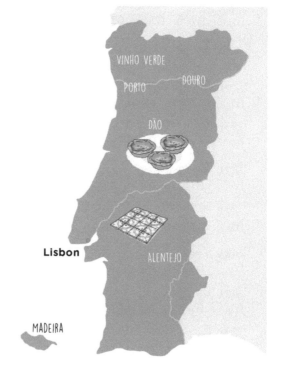

READING A PORTUGUESE WINE LABEL

Portugal follows EU standards for its wine labels. Here are some of the more common Portuguese label terms:

Adega: Winery

Casta: Grape variety

Colheita: Vintage

Denominaçâo de Origem Controlada (DOC): Highest quality wine, from a region with the strictest standards

Engarrafado/Garrafado: Bottled by

Garrafeira: Wine cellar. This term is regulated and used on white wines aged at least six months each in barrel and bottle, and red wines at least two years in barrel and one year in bottle.

Indicaçâo de Proveniencia Regulamentada (IPR): Regional wine

Produzido: Produced by

Quinta: Farm. It usually refers to an estate vineyard and winery

Vinho Branco: White wine

Vinho de Mesa: Table wine

Vinho Regional: Country wine

Vinho Reserva: A vintage wine with aging and minimum alcohol level requirements

Vinho Rosado: Rosé wine

Vinho Tinto: Red wine

Vinhas Velhas: Old vines

It often happens that countries that produce great wines are also great tourist destinations; and anyone who's ever munched on grilled octopus while sipping Vinho Verde at an outdoor café in Porto can tell you that the small but mighty Portugal manages to succeed at being both. With its centuries-old olive trees and bustling port cities (plus being the biggest cork producer in the world), Portugal is a wine-and-food paradise.

Viticulture was likely brought to Portugal during Roman occupation, and the country has long-standing traditions that date back to that time, including foot-treading grapes in shallow *lagares* vats. Some producers in the Alentejo region still make wine using ancient *talhas de barro*, clay amphorae that can measure up to seven feet tall and weigh a literal ton. Portugal has been at the wine law game longer than almost any other country, with Port vineyards having been protected and regulated since 1757.

Despite its diminutive size (it doesn't even crack the top 100 countries worldwide in land mass), Portugal boasts an incredible amount of cultural, geographic, and climatic diversity within its borders, a situation that is mirrored in its wines. Portugal's grapes evolved in near isolation, and it now grows nearly 250 indigenous varieties, second only to Italy.

VINHO VERDE

This northern Portuguese region is among the wetter and greener areas of the country. While some red and sparkling wine is made there, Vinho Verde (literally, "green wine") is best known for citric, zesty (and often, slight spritzy) white wines made from blends based on the Alvarinho grape that are ideal for summer sipping.

PORTO

Fortified Port wine derives its name from the town of Porto, where they are aged, rather than for the dizzying, steep slopes of the Douro river where its grapes are grown. These powerful, potent wines are Portugal's most famous export, blended from several grapes (usually Touriga Franca, Tinta Roriz, Tinta Barroca, Touriga Nacional, and Tinta Cão, but a whopping 82 varieties are allowed). They offer flavors and aromas of dried fruits, roasted nuts, and caramel, depending on the style. Port is best served for dessert, though some drier versions can be found (such as in "White" Port, made using only white grapes).

DOURO

It makes sense that the indigenous grape varieties that make Port should also make excellent dry wines, and that's exactly what can be found in the Douro. Douro reds are often delicious, with brambly red fruit flavors, pepper spice notes, and a chewy mouthfeel. Its white wines, while not easy to find, can be heady and complex.

DÃO

Mountainous and temperate, the Dão region has been gaining converts to its unique wines for the last decade. The reds tend to be tannic and bold, but what's even more exciting is the Dão's growth in white wine production, driven primarily by the standout Encruzado grape (which gives floral, fruity, and flinty aromas).

ALENTEJO

This southern area couldn't be more different than Vinho Verde. Abundantly sunny, warm, and experiencing some of the lowest rainfall totals in Europe, the Alentejo specializes in big, juicy, full-bodied wines. Several international varieties thrive there, and the region is doing exciting things with indigenous grapes like Antão Vaz and Touriga Nacional. But its most promising variety might be the tangy, red-fruited French cross Alicante Bouschet, which loves the Alentejo sunshine.

MADEIRA

I can confess to being a full-on Madeira fanboy. When I started my personal wine journey, I incorrectly assumed that *everyone* knew the nearly inde-structible fortified wines from this Portuguese island, given that they were the preferred drink of the US founding fathers. These wines are found in single-variety versions, in levels of increasing sweetness: Sercial, Verdelho, Bual (or Boal), and Malvasia. They are powerful, evoking Madeira's dramatic sea-cliff landscapes and often aged for decades in large oak vats, imparting notes of dried figs and nuts. Some still taste great after a full century of aging, and there's no better match for pecan pie!

Take a Tour of Portugal

Portugal's climatic diversity makes it an exceptional region for a tasting journey.

Quinta da Aveleda Vinho Verde (Vinho Verde)
A great introduction to Northern Portugal's signature style of floral and friendly Loureiro blended with Alvarinho, this is an immediately pleasurable white wine. It has a lemon color and smells like lemons, too. A hint of sweetness, good body, and ample cantaloupe flavors make it a great choice for summer picnics.

Quinta dos Roques Encruzado (Dão)
Medium-bodied and light-gold in color, this white wine is a Dão specialty, with notes of peaches, saline, and a mineral quality. In the mouth, white peach and cream flavors make it almost irresistible.

Prats & Symington Post Scriptum de Chryseia (Douro)
Port powerhouse Symington dry red offers a sophisticated take on the red Port grapes Touriga Franca and Touriga Nacional. Deep purple in the glass, its black pepper and leather aromas lead to a rich, plummy texture in the mouth.

Warre's Otima 10 Year Tawny Port (Porto)
Aged an average of ten years in the barrel, this fortified Tawny Port takes its name from its amber color. You'll get notes of fig, dried sour cherries, hazelnuts, and baking spices, and a powerful body that's lifted by great acidity. Serve it with a slight chill (and an open afternoon schedule).

Herdade Do Esporão Reserva White (Alentejo)
An Alentejo institution, crafting olive oil and hosting an award-winning restaurant, Esporão, this is the largest wine producer in the region. Their Reserva White (usually an Antão Vaz–based blend that differs each vintage) offers a lot of class for the money. You'll find orange blossom and oak spice notes, along with a full palate, ripe flavors of peaches and apricots, and a deep lemon color.

Blandy's 5 Year Old Medium Rich Bual (Madeira)
Aged for an average of five years in American oak casks, Blandy's (still owned by the family that founded the company in the 1800s) offers what might be the perfect introduction to the sweeter styles of Madeira's famous fortified wine. Dark bronze in color, with a spicy nose and medium-sweet profile, this wine can usher in dessert with its toffee, vanilla, and dried fig flavors.

Other Wine-Producing Areas of Note

The wine world extends far beyond the countries profiled in this chapter. Here are introductions to a few more noteworthy nations that just might be making your next favorite wine, waiting for you to discover.

AUSTRIA

Heavily influenced by Germany (and using similar labeling laws), this northern European country is a white wine specialist. Over 65 percent of its output is white, a third of which is dedicated to the racy and aromatic Grüner Veltliner (of which Austria is the world's leading producer). Its most famous wine areas are Kamptal and Wachau, near the Danube river. Apart from Grüner Veltliner, steely Rieslings and sparkling (Sekt) wines are also made, along with lighter-bodied, spicy reds from Zweigelt, Blaufränkisch, and Pinot Noir.

HUNGARY

This Central European country was once famous for creating the wine preferred by royalty worldwide: the botrytized dessert wine Tokaji Aszú. More recently, the "Bull's Blood" red wine blends of Eger saw increased popularity. The new renaissance for Hungarian wine, however, is coming by way of the white Furmint grape, which is being made into some of the most expressive, versatile, and exciting white wines in all of Europe.

SOUTH AFRICA

South Africa has been making wine since the 1650s, and at one point the sweet wines of Constantia (near Cape Town) were coveted throughout Europe. While those sweet wines are still made (and can be amazing), South Africa is best known for its dry wines. These include herbal, vegetal Sauvignon Blanc whites; intriguing, full-bodied Pinotage reds; and creamy, floral, and tropical Chenin Blanc whites. South Africa's warm climate is moderated in spots by cool breezes from the Western Cape, helping make rich wines that maintain freshness.

GREECE

Greece's winemaking history dates back nearly 6,500 years, making it one of the oldest wine-producing countries. In modern times, Greece has reinvented its wine market, often blending indigenous grapes with international varieties (especially on the island of Crete). Wine is made throughout Greece's territories, with soft, juicy Agiorgitiko reds from Nemea (in the Peloponnese) being a standout. Some of Greece's most complex and fresh white wines can be found on the gorgeous Naoussa island of Santorini, made from old vine Assyrtiko grapes.

CANADA

Canada is home to many wines, most of which are made in Ontario and British Columbia. When planted near sources of water, the cold Canadian climate can be moderated, which allows Chardonnay, Pinot Noir, and Cabernet Franc to ripen. Canada's specialty, however, is Icewine, a fresh, sweet delight made from frozen grapes. Canada makes more Icewine than all other countries *combined*. Generally, the hearty Vidal grape is used, though Riesling and even Cabernet Franc Icewines can be found. These are difficult to make, and therefore expensive, but can be intense, unforgettable wine experiences.

The Okanagan Valley in British Columbia is one of Canada's most promising—and beautiful—wine-producing areas.

Further Tasting Explorations

One of the best things about wine is that it is intimately tied to the place in which it is made. In this tasting, we expand your global exploration, venturing into styles and grapes that are signatures of other exciting areas in the wine world.

Langenlois Lois Grüner Veltliner (Kamptal, Austria)

Lois (rhymes with "choice") is one of the best all-around Grüners to try. Greenish-yellow in the glass, its aromas of spice and apple mingle with citrus and vegetable notes. Thanks to Austria's cooler climate, it's light and refreshing and finishes with green apple and lemon flavors.

Disznókő Dry Furmint (Tokaji, Hungary)

Long used in the fabled sweet wines of Tokaji, the Furmint grape is gaining attention for creating modern, fresh, and exciting dry white wines. This greenish-yellow example from Disznókő is boisterously aromatic, with citrus and white blossom notes, and lovely flavors of quince and pears. The palate is fresh, full of mineral-like qualities, and delightfully easy to drink.

Indaba Chenin Blanc (Western Cape, South Africa)

Yellow-gold in color, this is an unoaked, clean-as-a-whistle take on Chenin Blanc, with melon, kiwi, and lemon aromas. Those melons also come through on the palate, which is medium-bodied (a result of the area's moderate growing seasons) but balanced by a sense of crispness.

Kouros Agiorgitiko (Nemea, Greece)

Dark reddish-purple on the outside and full-bodied in the mouth, this is a great "starter" Agiorgitiko, a promising red grape from mainland Greece. Vanilla, toasted nut, dried herbs, and plums come across the nose, with juicy blackberry flavors and spices coming through with each sip.

Jackson Triggs Vidal Icewine (Niagara Peninsula, Canada)

This pale amber nectar is one of the most affordable of Canada's dessert wines, made from tiny quantities of frozen grapes that are picked and pressed in bone-chilling temperatures. It's intense, lush, and fresh, with ultra-pure aromas of tropical fruits and just a hint of caramel. While the ripe apricot flavors and mouthfeel are rich, the wine's fine acidity cuts through, keeping the palate refreshing despite its stratospheric sugar content.

CHAPTER 5

PLANNING YOUR OWN WINE TASTINGS

When it comes to learning about wine, the good news is the same as the bad news: wine is a complicated topic, and there's no magic shortcut to learning about it.

That's both daunting and liberating. In a very real sense, it's hard to get started with wine, because there's so much breadth and depth to the subject. But that's also what makes it so incredibly fun. Wine as a topic is so big that you can spend a lifetime exploring it and never exhaust the possibilities.

In endless potential, however, there are near-endless pitfalls. To navigate the immense ocean of wine tasting, you're going to need a map. That's where having a wine tasting plan comes into play.

Picking a Theme

One of the best ways to begin your wine tasting journey is by organizing tastings into structured learning experiences. That structure comes via tasting several wines within a set theme that logically connects them.

Thankfully, wine tasting lends itself to an almost infinite set of such possible themes. Want to learn about a particular country, or region? How about a certain grape variety? Or a style of wine? Or wines meant for a specific dinner course, such as dessert? When it comes to tasting themes, you're really only limited by your imagination and your bank account.

Here are a few thematic tasting threads, to get you going:

- One grape variety from different countries or regions

- One grape variety from the same country or region

- One grape made in different styles (dry to sweet, rosé to red, sparkling and still)

- A single wine style (sparkling, fortified, dessert)

- Different wines from a single region (Italy, Portugal, and France are great places to start, as they have so many distinct regional differences)

- Off-the-beaten-path grapes (i.e., grapes other than the ubiquitous Chardonnay, Cabernet Sauvignon, Merlot, etc.).

- Vertical (the same wine, across multiple vintages)

- Horizontal (different producers' wines from the same grape/region, from the same vintage)

- Blind tastings (more on this on page 163)

- Wines from a similar price bracket (e.g., all under $15, or all over $25)

- Regional wine dinners (try wines from a particular region with food recipes from that same area, like Rioja with tapas)

Don't underestimate how powerful a themed tasting can be. Comparing similar items within a connecting framework is one of *the* most effective ways to learn about any topic. This is basically the same method that I used to up my tasting IQ exponentially when I first started learning about wine, so I know how well it works.

Budget Wine Picks: Value at $10 and Under

Wine needn't be expensive, of course, to be good. Because of intense competition in the global wine marketplace, you can now find wines that are true to their regions and grapes, and are fault-free and tasty, for great prices. Here are some picks that combine easy drinking, deliciousness, and wallet-friendliness.

Freixenet Cordon Negro Brut (Cava, Spain)

With this sparkler, you get the Champagne method of production, but without the enormous price tag. A creamy palate that ends with refreshing acidity, apple and ginger aromas, and flavors of pear are all wrapped up here in a lovely, light gold presentation that's easy to imbibe.

Chateau Ste. Michelle Gewürztraminer (Columbia Valley, Washington State)

This off-dry white wine is a perennial winner, with rose petal, lychee, and clove notes and flavors of stone fruits and tangerines. Pair this light gold sipper with spicy foods, as its slight sweetness and round palate will help cool off the spices' heat.

Mulderbosch Cabernet Sauvignon Rosé (Stellenbosch, South Africa)

It's tough to tame Cabernet Sauvignon into a tasty rosé, but this producer manages to do it on the cheap. Medium-bodied and fresh in the mouth, with a pale rose color, this has just a hint of candied red fruits. The flavors evoke pomegranates, while the nose will remind you of grapefruit and strawberries.

Cono Sur 'Bicicleta' Pinot Noir (Central Valley, Chile)

Purple-red in color and extremely friendly in demeanor, this is a consistent value Pinot Noir that's often on sale for under $10. Red berry flavors, hints of smoke and baking spices, and a well-rounded but refreshing palate all combine in a style that's surprisingly well-balanced for the price.

Ravenswood Vintners Blend Zinfandel (California, United States)

Violet in the glass, medium-bodied in the mouth, and full of brambly spice on the nose, this is one of the more classic—and delicious—examples of California red Zin. It smells juicy, with all of those raspberry jam aromas, and it tastes even juicier, with plum and boysenberry flavors.

Choosing the Wines

Obviously, choosing wines for your tasting is contingent on your theme. Once you're set on a theme to guide your tasting, you can start to explore options within it for specific wine selections. You're going to want a budget, either in total or per bottle, because wine buying can be exciting and can get pretty expensive, pretty quickly.

When I decided to start exploring the world of wine, I often visited a wine shop that was on the way home from one of my long commuting drives. Each week, I set a budget and decided on a theme, for example, Bordeaux blends under $20 a bottle. I knew nothing about wine regions or most of the grapes, so I decided to do comparative tastings, as long as I didn't blow my budget. That time remains one of the fondest in my memory of my personal wine journey, even now after having visited many of the beautiful places that I'd only dreamed of back then, because I was learning with every sniff and sip, and that's just *fun* to do.

Back then, we didn't have the same volume of instantly available online information that we can access now with a quick Internet search. Wine buying might seem daunting because we're overwhelmed by choices, but a few quick Internet searches are often all you need to whittle down your choices considerably; and this can even be done *while* you're shopping. You'll find several wine review options online to help you narrow your selections; often, a Google search on wine styles or specific wines will return an aggregated score (right within the search results) from consumer-review website CellarTracker.com, which can help steer you toward good buys (and steer you away from potentially subpar purchases).

I strongly suggest beginning simply and modestly when planning your first tastings: set your sights on widely available grape varieties (such as Chardonnay, Cabernet Sauvignon, Sauvignon Blanc) and/or broader regions (e.g., Mendoza in Argentina, Sonoma County in California, or Provence in France). These will provide you with more options, at lower overall costs, and help you build up your tasting chops before tackling individual appellations (like Burgundy or Napa Valley), more esoteric varieties (Chenin Blanc, anyone?), or specific vintages, all of which increase the time, focus, and cost involved in tasting and evaluating them. Remember that patience is one of the main virtues when it comes to learning about wine (with most of the fun being in the journey itself, since that means that we get to drink!).

My Go-To Wine Picks

In this tasting, I share some of the wines that I love to drink myself. They're not the highest rated or most expensive wines that I've reviewed; they're just delicious and keep me coming back again and again.

Schramsberg Brut Rosé (North Coast, California)

Not cheap, but also a good buy compared to the wines against which it competes: $50-and-up bubbles from Champagne. I used to drink so much of this that I referred to it as the Roberts House Pour. A pale salmon in the glass, there's complexity in all of the vibrant fruit aromas (citrus, apples, red berries), along with bread and toast notes. Sour cherry and strawberry flavors dance on a palate that is refreshing but also feels luxurious and elegant.

Schloss Johannisberg Riesling Feinherb 'Gelblack' (Rheingau, Germany)

I adore the steely, austere—yet approachable—Rieslings from the Rheingau region and have been lucky enough to visit there many times. This wine takes me right back to my memories of walking the Rhine river's vineyards. Schloss Johannisberg has over 1,200 years of history behind it, so they've got a great story, too. The light palate is boosted by ample acidity, with some sugar to give it roundness. Greenish-gold hues are followed by white flower, lime, lemon, pear, and ginger notes and then flavors of white peaches and quince. Simply delicious!

Ramey Chardonnay (Sonoma County, California)

I don't know anyone who doesn't like this wine. A lovely yellow-gold color, with complex aromas of white flowers, lemon curd, hazelnuts, and citrus, the palate is at once rich and vibrant, with white peach, lemon zest, citrus, and toast flavors. It also ages beautifully, and so makes for a great gift for both the patient and impatient white wine drinkers in your life.

Donnafugata 'Sedara' Nero d'Avola (Sicily, Italy)

This garnet-colored wine is made with Nero d'Avola, which is a bit like the Cabernet Sauvignon of Sicily. It's floral and juicy on the nose, and spicy, too, with dark fruit flavors and a palate that's got good body, but also enough acidity to pair with hearty pasta dishes.

THE IMPORTANCE OF FINDING A GOOD WINE STORE

Often the most important resource you can access when shopping for wines is a knowledgeable staff at a reputable wine store (or in the wine department of larger stores). These fine folks can be indispensable, in that they have intimate knowledge of their inventory and can steer you toward alternatives within your price range if the first choice on your wine shopping list isn't available. I've had great wine store staff turn me on to lesser-known wine regions, or new brands, many of which have become personal favorites through the years.

Look for stores with good online reviews, and ask to speak with someone from their staff to help you find a wine when you go in to shop. That will give you a quick litmus test as to their knowledge and helpfulness and help you establish a relationship with them. An experienced wine store staff can act almost like a personal sommelier, once they get to know your wine tastes. Similarly, for international wines that you enjoy, it's helpful to check the back label for details on the importer, as many smaller- and medium-sized import companies build their portfolio around similar tastes and so may have similar wines to try. In some cases, like the famous and well-regarded Kermit Lynch Wine Merchant in Berkeley, the shop carries the wines that they import.

Setting Up the Tasting

Executing a tasting is where the *real* fun begins. Like picking a tasting theme, the scope of the tasting is only limited by your logistics and your budget. Having said that, some guidelines are in order, since we're dealing with a product that isn't all that inexpensive on average and contains anywhere from 10 to 15 percent alcohol.

Treat your first tastings as experiments, allowing you to learn not only about the wines and how to taste, but also providing experience that will allow you to tweak future tastings to make them even better. Start small, either on your own or with three to five guests. Going beyond five total tasters starts to complicate matters in terms of stemware, number of bottles of each wine required, space to accommodate all of the tasters, and the like. These are conquerable challenges, of course, but if you're just starting out, they can be a distraction from your wine learning.

There are advantages to inviting like-minded friends to share in your first tastings. Having differing opinions and differing impressions of the same wine can help everyone involved pick up on nuances that a lone taster might miss at first. You can spread the cost of the tasting around, making it more economical, and guests can propose future creative theme ideas. It can also be a blast to go shopping for the wines together, or to be pleasantly surprised by the selections that each guest contributes to the tasting theme.

The tasting itself will take some preparation. First, you'll want to get the wines close to their ideal temperatures (see Serving Temperatures on page 169). That might require chilling sparkling, white, or rosé wines, or letting red wines warm slightly. It's a good idea to set up half as many glasses as there are wines to taste, and provide a bucket (or similar vessel) to be used to dump leftover wine, and/or to be used as a spittoon for those who would prefer not to swallow all of the wines as they taste. This allows glasses to be reused (you can rinse out the glass with a small amount of the next wine in the tasting, which can be dumped into the bucket before pouring a full sample of that next wine). Minimizing the number of glasses also gives you room on the table to write about your impressions of each wine in your journal as you taste them. (Trust me, trying to do this in your lap with a table full of stemware totally sucks.)

BLIND TASTING

Few wine experiences are as humbling as a blind tasting. When English wine pro Harry Waugh was asked whether he had ever confused a Bordeaux with a Burgundy, his now-famous reply was "Not since lunch!" Blind tastings help reduce potential bias in wine evaluation and are an essential component of judging wine competitions worldwide.

After you get a few tastings under your belt, a blind tasting will remind you of how much you still *don't* know about wine, and you will often be surprised at which wine turns out to be your favorite in a blind lineup. (This is a great way to turn yourself on to a wine or brand that you previously wouldn't have considered.)

To pull off a blind tasting, you can have each tasting guest bring a "secret" wine and designate someone (who will know the identities of the wines) to put each bottle into long paper bags and do the pouring. After tasting all the wines, the best part comes when everyone declares their personal favorites (and why) and the identity of each wine is revealed.

A quick note on spitting: this is absolutely acceptable behavior during a wine tasting, so don't be afraid to do it. It's a good idea to spit and/or dump wines as you taste them, rather than drink them all, so that your head is clear enough to evaluate and learn as you progress through the tasting (even when spitting, you will still absorb some alcohol through the interior of your mouth). You can always go back to your favorites after the tasting and drink up the ones that you like after you've taken notes.

A good number of wines to have on the table when starting out is two to three, tasted and discussed one at a time. This gives a chance for everyone to return to previous wines and compare them, and allows the discussion to flow freely while still focusing it on one wine at a time, with a break between each set of wines. There are about 25 ounces in a 750ml bottle of wine, so you can pour about six glasses if you keep each pour to four ounces each. This is an easy method to remember, and it's also easy to "eyeball" without having to break out the measuring cups.

For some reason, pouring wine into glasses in front of others seems to send people into states of near-panic nervousness. Having a small mat under each set of glasses helps with cleanup if there are any spills. Your best bet, though, is to employ the professional's pouring technique: when nearing the finish of a pour, gently twist the bottle in your hand as you raise the neck to stop pouring. This technique will eliminate almost all of the drips that come with pouring a wine. (And from this day onward, you'll be amazed at how many restaurant servers *don't* do this.)

PREPARING THE WINES

Once you are ready to pull off a tasting, there are some things you'll want to do to make sure each wine has a fair shot when you taste and evaluate it.

Sparkling, white wines, and rosé wines—basically, any wines that you have to chill—should be poured just before you taste them (within a few minutes of when you want to start putting them into your mouth). They should still have a chill on them when you take your first sip and can be revisited and retasted as they warm in the glass, to appreciate how they develop.

You'll want to pour most red wines several minutes *before* tasting them, to allow them to interact with the air and reveal themselves aromatically first. This is especially true for very young red wines from recent vintages; if they are wines made for bottle aging, then they will likely be a bit closed-off at first, only starting to show their stuff after several minutes of air exposure.

Decanting these wines to expose them to air before serving can help. (You can buy a decanter or wine aerator, or you can just pour the wine into a pitcher.)

The exception to this is older vintages of wines (red or white). In almost all instances, older wines are more fragile than younger wines, as more of their internal structure and natural preservatives (like tannins) have already broken down. They will degrade more quickly in the presence of air than their younger counterparts, and so should be opened and poured just before tasting them.

Older red wines and younger unfiltered wines often have harmless sediment that settles into the bottom of the bottle. For those wines, a bit of decanting can help; slowly pour the wine into the decanter, taking care to stop pouring when you see sediment getting close to the neck of the bottle. This will help ensure that your wine tasting doesn't include anything literally chewy in the glass!

DETERMINING THE ORDER OF WINES

Wine tasting order is important. While it doesn't have to be *perfect*, if the sequence is unbalanced, you won't get the most out of each wine in the lineup. That's because your palate is like a muscle, in that it can get exhausted from tasting and needs recovery time (anywhere from a few minutes to a couple of hours). In the wine industry, we call this "palate fatigue," and it can make wines start to taste similar or dull. This can happen if you taste a sweet wine before

Following the right order is one of the most important aspects of any organized tasting.

a dry one, or sip a full-bodied, powerfully alcoholic red before a lighter-bodied white. To keep your palate from getting wiped out, taste wines in the following order (as much as reasonably possible), and take breaks when needed:

- White to red

- Lighter-bodied to fuller-bodied

- Lower alcohol to higher alcohol

- Drier to sweeter

RECORDING YOUR THOUGHTS

For each wine that you taste, note your impressions; if in a group, get everyone to contribute their individual thoughts on each wine tasted. Consider leaving out a glass of the previous wine if you'd like to do a comparison. Here are some questions to ask yourself as you taste through each glass:

- What colors and hues does the wine present in the glass?

- What are the primary flavors and aromas? Are they strong, or do they require more concentration to pick them out?

- Are there other, more subtle notes coming in the nose or the flavors of the wine?

- Do the aromas change over time as the wine warms and is exposed to more air in the glass? If so, what new aromas are present?

- How does the wine feel in your mouth? Is it light, heavy, powerful, elegant? What feelings does it evoke? Do the elements feel harmonious, or do certain aspects stand out more at different times?

- Does the wine have a finish? How long is it, and what's on it? Is it consistent with the flavors and aromas, or does it offer something new? Is the finish enjoyable?

- Do you like it? Hate it? Try to express *why* you feel that way after tasting it. This step is instrumental in helping you later identify similar wines that you may want to try (or want to avoid).

Wine Glasses

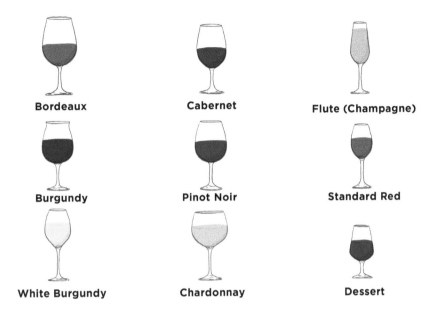

Bordeaux	Cabernet	Flute (Champagne)
Burgundy	Pinot Noir	Standard Red
White Burgundy	Chardonnay	Dessert

Much fuss has been made in the wine business about the "proper" stemware for tasting wine, most of it by companies that sell stemware. If you wanted, you could literally buy a separate type of wine glass for every wine style or major wine grape variety. In my opinion, that would be an enormous waste of most people's cash.

Both the wine world and the scientific community have tried to determine how much of a tasting difference those specialized glasses actually make. Research published in the *Journal of Sensory Studies* found that specialized wine glasses did have an impact on aroma perception, but that impact was subtle. Similarly, a Tokyo Medical and Dental University study employed a unique experiment, showing that the same wine presented different bouquets and finishes when sipped from different stemware. How well most people pick up on these differences, however, is debatable.

What's my take after years of following this thorny topic? If you find yourself primarily drinking one style of wine, or mostly wines made from a single variety or region, then a specialized glass might be just the ticket for you. After all, they are designed to enhance how you perceive that particular style of wine that you're so fond of drinking, and even a subtle impact might make a difference to you. In those cases, it's more of an investment in your future pleasure (just don't forget your checkbook, because some of those glasses don't come cheap).

For everyone else, we can get by with exactly *one* type of wine glass. Yes, for almost every type of wine. Yes, even for bubbles.

Here's the magic formula: you want a tulip-shaped wine glass that can hold 12 to 14 ounces of wine, with a rim that's as thin as you can comfortably stand without fear that you'll break it.

A tulip-shaped glass of that size will handle almost any style of wine (with the exception of fortified wines, which need a smaller pour and thus a smaller glass) admirably. The bowl shape allows the right amount of contact with air (to release a wine's volatile aromatic compounds), while the thin rim will deposit the wine onto your tongue with minimal impact. (Thicker rims can splash the wine into your mouth; while subtle, this can have a negative effect on how you perceive the wine's texture.) Shape more or less trumps everything else, and you can find several acceptable options to fit almost any budget. If you need any additional validation, keep in mind that I primarily review wines—professionally—in wine glasses that I bought at my local Target.

Wine Storage

Like wine glasses, wine storage is an oft-debated topic among wine wonks worldwide. Fortunately, the basics are extremely simple. Like most fine foods, the enemies of wine are light, heat, and vibration. Keep your wine away from those, and storage—in terms of protecting the flavor and drinkability of your wine—shouldn't be much more than a space problem.

This means that, aside from a sun-facing windowsill next to a train station in a hot climate, about the worst place you can store your wine is in that built-in wine rack above your refrigerator. The vibration and heat emanating from the appliance will absolutely shorten the lifespan of the wine being stored above it.

Most wine that you buy isn't meant to be aged more than a year or so in the bottle, so if you're planning on tasting the wines you buy relatively soon, then you shouldn't sweat storage too much. Almost any dark place will do, provided that the temperature doesn't fluctuate wildly. This is why we see so many wines stored in cellars and basements: it's dark; there's usually some humidity (helping prevent corks from drying out, which is also why you see wines stored on their sides rather than upright, the wine helping keep the cork moist as well); and the temperature, if it does change, moves in slow arcs with the seasons (rather than spiking up or down, which is bad for wine chemistry).

For those who live in an apartment, or in a home without a basement, longer-term wine storage is a bit trickier. If you find yourself craving a fancy wine refrigerator, whether out of necessity or desire, you'll find no shortage of styles, sizes, and brands. You'll want to focus on models that are specifically designed for wine storage, from brands that focus on wine (rather than on cooling in general). These will take into account the proper storage temperatures, minimize vibration from the unit itself, and have some method for recapturing humidity.

HOW TO CHILL WINE LIKE A PRO

Here's a handy pro tip to get your white, sparkling, or rosé wine to the right serving temperature in no time. Grab a bucket, some ice, and a bit of table salt. Fill the bucket about halfway with ice, then pour in some cold water, and sprinkle in the salt. You want just enough water and ice that it covers three quarters of the wine bottle when placed inside the bucket. This will have your wine chilled to a perfect serving temperature in under fifteen minutes. It works so well because the water increases the surface area for the ice's chilling effect, making it more efficient, while the salt lowers the freezing point of the mixture, increasing the ice water's ability to absorb warmer energy from the wine bottle (reducing the total cooling time required).

SERVING TEMPERATURES

The "correct" serving temperature for particular types of wine is more about avoiding problems than it is about finding the "perfect" exact temperature for each wine's flavors. Wines that are too cold will smell and taste dull; those that are too warm will have their alcohol accentuated in unpleasant ways. As much as possible, you want to be able to taste the wines as the winemakers intended, and getting them within a recommended temperature range can help.

Here's a quick guide to serving temperatures, by wine style.

- Sparkling wines and lighter dessert wines: 40 to 50 degrees Fahrenheit ("ice cold")

- White wines, rosés, and fortified wines: 50 to 60 degrees Fahrenheit ("chilled")

- Red wines: 60 to 70 degrees Fahrenheit ("cellar temperature")

Note that nothing trumps your personal tastes, so if you prefer your red wines a bit cooler, then by all means do what works for you. Just bear in mind that serving a wine style outside those temperature ranges might give you an impression of the wine that's different than what the producer intended.

CHILL YOUR SPARKLER FOR SAFETY'S SAKE

You want sparkling wine to be ice cold when you open it, as this minimizes the chance for injury when removing the cork. While it sounds amusing, it's actually no laughing matter: a sparkling wine cork can reach 50 miles per hour as it leaves the bottle—fast enough to break things or take an eye out. So, before opening that bubbly, make sure the bottle is well chilled; this slows down the carbonation, which is what can propel the cork with dangerous force. If you like your bubbles a bit warmer, it's best to let that warming happen *after* the bottle has been opened.

To open your sparkling wine, first remove the wire cage on the neck of the bottle by twisting the tab until the cage loosens. Then, cover the neck with a small towel, point the bottle away from anything (or anyone) that could get damaged from a flying cork, and hold the cork in one hand while—slowly—twisting the bottle with the other hand. Apply gentle pressure against the cork as it starts to release, slowing its progress so that it comes out with a gentle "pfffft" rather than with a loud, messy "pop!"

Optimal Serving Temperatures

40-50°F   50-60°F   60-70°F

LEFTOVER WINE

If you plan on opening several bottles for a tasting, be prepared to deal with the wine lover's universal dilemma: leftover wine. Storing leftover wine that you plan on finishing off in the next few days is pretty easy: simply put the cork back into the bottle (or use a special closure/cap if you're dealing with sparkling wines), and put the bottle into the fridge. You'll get a good two to three days of additional drinking from almost any wine using this method.

Storing leftover wine for longer than a few days presents larger challenges. There are so many gadgets available for this type of storage that it's almost as confusing a market as buying the wine itself. On the budget end, there are vacuum-pump-style systems, which work by removing air from the bottle, minimizing oxidation to make the leftover wine last longer. I find that the stoppers for these systems tend to lose grip over time, so they are best for shorter-term leftover storage. Single-use stopper systems, like the Repour Wine Saver, work by absorbing oxygen and can add a few more days of drinking to your leftovers (though as single-use, they tend to be less environmentally friendly). My personal favorite solution is the Savino, a stylish carafe that includes a float that protects the wine against oxygen; it's a bit pricier and only works on one wine at a time, but prolongs leftover wine quite well for several days when used correctly.

At the high end of wine preservation is the Coravin, which works by pulling wine from the bottle directly through the cork closure via a needle, replacing whatever wine is displaced with inert gas. Theoretically, this means that the wine remaining in the bottle (which technically hasn't been opened) can last indefinitely (or, at least as long as storage conditions allow). It's an expensive solution, best left to serious collectors who want to sample wines as they develop over many years in the bottle.

Food and Wine

White wine with fish, red wine with meat, right? Hang on a minute. While that popular pairing advice is a time-honored starting point, it's by no means the end of the story. Pairing wine with food doesn't need to be complicated, but there's more to it than just matching a wine style with particular protein sources.

Let's take a deeper look at the basics of wine and food pairing and explore why some pairings work (and others don't).

ACIDITY

A ton of articles have been written telling us what wines to pair with, say, Thanksgiving dinner. Almost none of those articles explain *why* certain wines play nice at the dinner table with certain dishes. Wine pairing is, at best, an inexact art form; because our individual tastes vary, it's no easy task to find a wine and food match that can please everyone. There are, however, some basic guidelines that can seriously increase your potential for success when pairing up your vino and vittles.

When it comes to successful wine and food pairing, acidity—the lemon-like vibrancy of some wines that makes your mouth water—is your friend. Grapes that are naturally high in acids (such as Sauvignon Blanc and Riesling in whites, or Barbera, Pinot Noir, and Gamay for reds) will fare well with most fare. This works under the same principle as adding a spritz of lemon juice to food. Acidity makes your mouth water, cuts through fatty richness, and helps emphasize a sense of freshness by breaking down fats, proteins, and carbohydrates.

SYNC WITH THE SAUCE

Another food and wine pairing guideline is minding what's on top of your food. Sauces matter when it comes to pairing, sometimes more than the ingredients themselves. Richer sauces often demand wines with richer textures to match them. For example, a buttery sauce will match up nicely with many oak-aged white wines.

Just as sauces change the weight and texture of a meal, so does the preparation style. A light salad or delicately prepared white fish will get clobbered by most red wines, while a slow-cooked roast will be so dense and flavorful that it can be paired with the biggest, burliest red that you can find.

Conversely, the more acidic the dish or its sauce (for example, adding a vinaigrette dressing), the lighter and more acidic you can go on the wine.

COMPLEMENT AND CONTRAST

Wine functions like another ingredient in a meal. In this way, a wine can either complement similar flavors and weights in the meal's ingredients, or pleasantly contrast dissimilar elements (by presenting opposites in texture and body).

An example of complementing would be lobster and potatoes in butter with a Chardonnay. Both have a sense of heaviness in the mouth, and both can show creamy flavors and consistency. Combined, these create a powerhouse of gustatory texture that builds into a delicious crescendo.

A contrast would be a salad topped with parmesan cheese paired with a lighter white wine, like Riesling. The acidity in the latter undercuts the fat of the cheese, refreshing your palate and getting you ready for the next bite (while matching one another in tanginess along the way).

Red wine has tannins that bind to protein, making it an ideal match for steak.

The Classic Pairing: Wine and Cheese

We've all heard that wine can be pure magic when paired with the right cheese. This is true, but it can be a bit of a challenge, because both cheese and wine can have complex flavors and textures. This tasting will help you get a handle on both (while going light on your bank account and wowing your taste buds at the same time).

Goat Cheese + Edna Valley Vineyard Sauvignon Blanc (Central Coast, California)

Goat cheese is at once creamy and piquant, so you need a wine that will both cut through the fattiness and stand up to the cheese's tanginess. This Sauvignon Blanc is a good choice; its lemon color is indicative of its zesty acidity (to handle the tanginess in the goat cheese). That vivacious palate will also slice through the cheese's creaminess, while its herbal nose will provide some extra complexity to the pairing.

Pepper Jack + Loosen Bros. 'Dr L.' Riesling (Mosel, Germany)

Monterey Jack and spicy peppers are a culinary match made in heaven but can be hell for many wines. Hot peppers can overemphasize a wine's alcohol, causing a burning sensation in your mouth. Off-dry German Rieslings are perfect for pepper, like this little gem from Loosen Bros. The lime-like acids will cut the milky richness of the jack, while the quince aromas and sweet lemon-drop flavor will help cool the pepper's burn.

Brie + Wente Vineyards Morning Fog Chardonnay (Livermore Valley, California)

Bloomy rind brie is the queen of cheese, an irresistible and affordable luxury. You'll want to pair it with a wine that is similarly indulgent; think big, fruity whites such as this Chardonnay from California. Wente's perennially good Morning Fog Chardonnay has a slight acidic bite to contrast with brie's milky texture, while having enough palate weight to match the cheese's decadence. The big, bold peach aromas and flavors will also contrast nicely with the brie's earthiness.

Sharp Cheddar + Kim Crawford Pinot Noir (Marlborough, New Zealand)

While it has heartiness, cheddar also has more nuanced flavors. So, it's best to avoid lots of tannin (the component that makes some red wines taste bitter), which can wreak havoc on cheddar's delicate side. Instead, go for something like this Pinot Noir from New Zealand. A gorgeous garnet in the glass, it's earthy and fresh, with tea-leaf notes and dark cherry and red berry flavors. More important, it's low in tannins and high on elegance.

Parmesan or Manchego + Ruffino Chianti (Tuscany, Italy)
Aged cheeses like Parmesan and Manchego are my personal favorites, because of their solid texture and bold flavors. These need simpler wine pairings to act as a supporting cast to their starring roles. They play quite nicely with many red wines, especially those with low tannins and higher acidic verve, like this Chianti from Tuscany. Hints of orange rind and sour cherry flavors act as a solid backdrop to all the earthy bedrock provided by the cheese.

Blue Cheese + Royal Tokaji Mád Cuvée Late Harvest Tokaji (Tokaj, Hungary)
Love-it-or-hate-it aromatic cheeses like blue are difficult to pair, as they can trample lighter wines (and some can taste metallic if matched with tannic wines). Sweet wines with ample acidity are a great match for blue, like this late harvest white blend from Hungarian producer Royal Tokaji. It has sweet, bold flavors of apple pie, honey, and apricot candy (to match the blue's boldness) with vibrant acidity (to balance the cheese's heaviness).

Wine + Food: Complement and Contrast

Complementing and/or contrasting is at the heart of successful wine and food pairing. You can use this technique with the flavors, textures, body, and weight of both the food and the wine. Here are a handful of examples for you to try.

Thai or Vietnamese Salad + 'Grooner' Grüner Veltliner (Niederösterreich, Austria)

These salads often have either tangy, zesty, and highly acidic dressings, or creamier dressings such as peanut sauce. This lemon-colored, entry-level Grüner is the perfect foil for that scenario: it will either match the acidity of the tangier dressings with its vibrant palate or contrast the creaminess of the heavier dressings by "cutting through" it. Additionally, the herbal aromas will complement the vegetable ingredients.

Sushi + Nino Franco Rustico Prosecco Superiore (Veneto, Italy)

Because sushi is often served with ginger and wasabi, you need some sweetness to counter its spicy heat, and fruity carbonation to offset the savory qualities of the salty fish. Enter Nino Franco's Rustico, an almost greenish-pale Italian Prosecco made in steel tanks to emphasize its fruity pear and apple aromas. Ripe peach flavors on the palate will handle those spicy sushi condiments with ease.

Steak + Condado de Haza Tinto (Ribera del Duero, Spain)

Since red wine tannins can soften the feel of protein in the mouth, they are a great choice for steak. Leaner cuts, like flank steak, can use a red that has tannin, but not too much tannin, like this garnet-colored, full-bodied Spanish Tempranillo. It has just enough structure to soften the flank steak's chewiness and enough ripe berry flavors and violet and spice aromas to counter the heavier flavors of the steak.

Fruit Tart + Domaine de Durban Muscat de Beaumes de Venise (Rhône Valley, France)

Desserts need wines that are sweeter than they are, otherwise, they tend to obliterate the taste of the wine in your mouth. Fruit tarts are a good pick to match with wines, since the acidity in the fruit counters some of their sweetness. This amber-gold dessert wine, made from Muscat Blanc à Petit Grains in France's Southern Rhône region, has apricot, mandarin orange, and citrus aromas to complement the fruits in the dessert. It also has a rich, sweet palate to match the dessert's texture.

TASTINGS INDEX

INDEX

ACKNOWLEDGMENTS

Thanks to Callisto Media for the opportunity and to Pam Kingsley in particular, who knows much more about editing than I do (and a lot more about wine than she thinks). Thanks also to Frank Voutsakis, not only a gifted writer in his own right, but also a philosophical drinking companion, and a handy legal expert. A tip of the glass to Chip Miller, who never stopped bugging me to write a book.

Special thanks to my love, Shannon, and my amazing kiddo, Lorelai, for their patience and support. Finally, thanks to you for reading, and cheers to those everywhere who raise a glass of vino mindfully.

ABOUT THE AUTHOR

Joe Roberts is a writer, blogger, video personality, wine critic, and frequent wine competition judge whose work has appeared in publications as varied as Playboy.com and *Parade*. He's best known as the iconoclastic voice behind 1winedude.com, one of the most awarded and influential wine blogs in the world, and is the author of *Wine Taster's Journal: Drink, Rate, Record, and Remember*. Joe makes his living traveling the globe uncovering off-the-beaten-path wine gems, as well as writing and talking about the world of wine and wine marketing. He lives near Philadelphia with his daughter, Lorelai. When his hands aren't in a notebook, at the keyboard, or holding a wine glass, he's playing bass guitar with the Steve Liberace Band.

CPSIA information can be obtained
at www.ICGtesting.com
Printed in the USA
JSHW031952170720
6715JS00003B/15

9 781646 119608